Clarke, a.k.a.,

Thank you brothe

For your love, friendship, support, encouragement
and help. I wish we could take you
to Oregon and plant you in whatever
church home we find. Thank you for
being a real friend and great reverend...

EPIC
HOPE

Finding the

Only Hope That

Can Heal Our

Deepest Hurts

EPIC
HOPE

JOEL HUGHES

EPIC Hope
Joel Hughes
Published by Rebekah's Hope Publications
23152 Verdugo Dr.
Suite 100
Laguna Hills, CA 92653
www.rebekahshope.org
contact@rebekahshope.org

Copyright © 2020 Joel Hughes
Our passion at Rebekah's Hope is to equip those fighting cancer, illness, and despair find hope and healing through our books, movie, and e-courses.

Edited by Lisa Guest
Book Design by Steven Plummer, http://spbookdesign.com/
Cover photo by Gavin Bragdon

Paperback: 978-1-7320919-4-8
eBook: 978-1-7320919-5-5

epic [**ep**-ik]

noun

A word, whose meaningful definition(s) and correct applications are now obscured and have been raped to death mostly by the 25-and-under crowd. It has been overused as "the" catchphrase used to describe a situation, person, event, movie, taking a sh#t, etc. The abuse and birth as a catchphrase has its origins among avid gamers and pretentious English majors. (urbandictionary.com)

epic [**ep**-ik]

noun

A long narrative poem written in elevated style, in which heroes of great historical or legendary importance perform valorous deeds. The setting is vast in scope, covering great nations, the world, or the universe, and the action is important to the history of a nation or people. (The New Dictionary of Cultural Literacy)

epic [**ep**-ik]

adjective

Extending beyond the usual or ordinary especially in size or scope. (Webster's)

despair [də'sper]

noun

The complete loss or absence of hope.

I lay in a nasty bed in a dank motel room. I was barely breathing... and I could barely move. Next to me stood an old wood table, pocked with cigarette burns from years of use by hundreds of shady people. Dozens and dozens of empty beer cans littered the room. The suffocating smell of cigarettes clogged the air. My phone was dead. I scrawled a note to my kids on a scrap of paper. I told them how much I loved them and how sorry I was. Tears ran down the sides of my face. I had been drunk for days. I hadn't eaten for days. I was severely dehydrated. My mouth was a desert. Each breath came... slowly... and small. I had my laptop next to me on the bed, prepared to make one last effort to throw it through the window. I had little strength, but I figured if I faded out, I could throw the computer through the window to get someone's attention... and then get help. I really thought I might just fall asleep and never wake up... and part of me wanted that.

—Me, Eight Years Ago

CONTENTS

INTRODUCTION

UP, UP, UP I went. No, no, no! I was turning sideways and couldn't bring it back. Not good. BANG!...Blackness.... Lights out.

I was 17, and I raced motocross on the local circuit. It was a normal practice session at StarWest MX Track in Southern California. It was a windy day, but I had been riding laps around the track, hitting the jumps, and having fun. Again, I hit the berm and squared off with the largest jump on the track which—up to that point—had given me no problems. But this time, as I flew off the lip of the jump, a gust of wind hit me, blowing me *and* the 200-pound bike sideways through the air. I landed that way, still on the bike, and I hit hard.

I blacked out for a few seconds. Yes, a concussion. When I came to, I knew I had to get off the track because I was right where other riders would land. But something was wrong. Very wrong. My wrist was tweaked in a 90-degree angle, clearly broken. And my left leg didn't feel right at all. Looking down I saw that my leg, at the middle of my thigh, was flipped over in an "L" shape. *Ooooohhhhh S####*****! My femur was broken in half. It felt super strange and—at first—it didn't hurt. I clearly remember grabbing my leg below the break and flipping my leg back into its normal alignment—all the while fearing that another bike would land on me. Using my elbows, I frantically dragged myself to the side of the track as onsite medics rushed over. This all happened within seconds, but it felt like forever.

I'll spare you the rest of the tragic details that involved the ER, my screaming like a girl as nurses held me down so the doctor could pull my leg back into place, passing out, waking up to see someone drilling a hole through my shinbone and putting a rod through it for traction (a mechanism for straightening broken bones), then passing out again. Later that evening, a surgeon put a titanium rod *inside* my femur bone to hold the two pieces together. Okay, okay, enough details. They're fun to tell... *now*.

Once my leg was stabilized, my biggest concern was how long I'd be out before I could start racing again. Motocross was my life. I remember the doctor telling me I would be out for at least a year. A year! As a 17-year-old punk, I just felt angry. No, pissed. *How stupid. This sucks. Whatever.* I'll do whatever I need to do to heal. Then I'm back on a bike.

First I was back at school. The first four months of my senior year in high school, I was on crutches, and I had a cast on my arm for six months. Once I hit the one-year mark—but against my doctor's wishes—I got a new bike and started practicing again. It felt good to be back riding, and soon I was ready to race again....

It was my first race back. *Red... yellow... green*—and the gate dropped. About 20 riders, full of adrenaline and out for blood, took off like a swarm of angry hornets. We hit that first turn, and I was about midpack. I could work with that. The first lap of a race is a free-for-all madhouse as adrenaline is peaking and each racer maneuvers to get ahead of everyone else. Mid-lap, I flew off a large jump with other riders around me midair. I clipped another bike and landed hard. And I landed wrong...

again. I felt that strange feeling again in my leg. *Nooooo!* Again, I had to get off the track ASAP. I crawled to the sideline and looked down at my leg. It was intact. Thank God. Wrist? Normal. I still felt that strange yet too-familiar broken feeling, but higher in my leg this time. *Ooooohhhhh S####****!* My hip was broken. I knew it. I just knew it. Again, onsite medics were around me right away. I looked fine, but I knew something had broken inside me. My friend's mom loaded me into her old Suburban, and we headed to the nearest hospital. This was in Lancaster, California, basically the middle of nowhere.

In the ER, after taking X-rays, the doctor came in and told me that my hip was broken. See, at the top of your femur, you have a hip ball? Yeah, I broke that off. When I landed off that jump, the titanium rod held my femur together but forced up to my hip all the pressure from the impact. Snap, crackle, POP! That hip ball popped right off.

Again, my greatest concern was when I could get back to the dirt. As I sat in that gloomy room, with my X-rays lit up all over the wall, the doctor said I'd be out for at least another year. *No!* My heart sank, and this time I started crying. I had so *hoped* that it would be a minor issue. *Another year...* I still had hopes of getting back to racing, so like a prisoner of my body, I did my year.

Would you believe that, after a year of recuperating, I got *another* bike and returned to the motocross track a third time? I did. But this time I realized during practice that I could no longer do the jumps. I'd fly up to the face of the jump, hit the brakes, and roll over the top. I had lost the ability to push myself through the fear. I also realized I was not invincible. I was very vincible! I sold my bike and my Ford Ranger. I bought a Camaro Z28 (the coolest car I've ever had) and a Macintosh computer system to learn graphic design. My parents were quite happy with that decision!

HUMANITY'S UNIVERSAL LANGUAGE

We all live with little hopes. We don't usually think much about them. In fact, sometimes we may not even know we had a specific hope until it's dashed.

One thing that's become clear to me, hope and hoping are crucial to life. We are *hope-hungry beings*. No matter who we are or what we believe, we all share the need for hope. As we'll explore in this book, hope and hoping come in varying degrees. Not all of us hope for the same things, not all of an individual's hopes are the same intensity, and not everyone has the *kind* of hope they need to get through the toughest times.

Some hopes energize us and enable us to take action. My deep desire to get back to racing energized me to do physical therapy and take care of myself as I waited for my body to heal. That goal of being back on a bike gave me hope, and that hope gave me power.

Think about times when you were single, or maybe you're single now. You hope that sooner rather than later you will find him or her—The One. This hope energizes you to get your butt in the gym, eat well, and dress in something other than sweats and that old "I Love LA" t-shirt. (You don't even know where that shirt came from, but you love it—and that love is… uh… way too obvious.) You also make sure you shower and smell good. You carry gum or mints with you at all times. (I always packed Chapstick too. Hey, you never know!) Hope of future love also empowers you to take risks and put yourself out there.

But other hopes, smaller ones, matter little if they come to pass or not. You hope to win the lottery (you won't, so give up now), you hope to pass a test in some class, you hope your team wins, and you hope the **Taco Bell** you just ate doesn't wreck you in the coming hours (it will, so give up now). These hopes carry little to no power over us, and whether or not they materialize doesn't really matter. Well, except maybe that Taco Bell hope.

In other scenarios we use the word *hope*, but in those contexts the meaning is more like *knowing*. You hope you make this free throw. You hope your muffins turn out well. You hope the mail shows up today. We base these types of hope on **inductive reasoning**:[1] we look at a routine or pattern from the past and, on that basis, generalize what will most likely happen in the future. You've sunk a 1000 free throws in the past, baked these muffins dozens of times, and never seen the mail person take a day off (except Sundays and every possible holiday there is). You don't know the future, but you're pretty sure that your prediction is correct.

Finally, still other hopes paralyze us with fear because we have little to no control over them. These are the big hopes. You hope your plane lands safely in a crazy storm. You hope your spouse wasn't serious when he/she said, "I want a divorce." You hope the stock market can rally back after it tanks. You hope your HIV test comes back negative. You hope the doctor says all your scans come back clean. You hope the oncologist can treat this kind of cancer. Yep, we got serious just now. Even if you're not "religious," these hopes for big things prompt "God, please. *Please*, God."

THE BLISS OF YOUTHFUL ARROGANCE

When I was 23 years old, I was in seminary, studying to become a pastor. I didn't grow up in a religious or **Christian** home, but it was a good and loving home. To give you a sneak preview of the next chapter, when I was 17 and racing motocross, I was also a racist skinhead covered with tattoos, including "WHITE PRIDE"

---

1 A variety of technical terms and names of people that may be unfamiliar to readers have been included in a glossary of terms near the end of this book. At their introduction into the text each word, phrase, or name is put in bold.

across my whole back. By age 25, however, I was a Christian pastor at an all Korean church! Yeah, we'll get there.

But at 23 I was a full-time student who went to school in the mornings and worked a graveyard shift as a security guard. A single dude, I rented a little upstairs room in a five-bedroom house in Tustin, California. It had rust red shag carpet throughout. The owner was a not-so-nice old widow named Jeri. Short and pudgy, with a snow-covered crew cut, she wore the same thing every day: knee-length jean shorts and an American flag t-shirt. She never talked to me; she preferred to communicate by slipping little notes under my door: "Your rent is past due"; "Don't park in the driveway"; and "You are not allowed to have anyone over." Her super odd skinny adult son lived in a room downstairs. He only came out of his dreary room to microwave a TV dinner, and then he would scuttle back into his dark lair. He didn't work—and he looked like he was straight out of the '70s. He never acknowledged my existence even if I were standing right next to him in the kitchen, and he was even crankier than old Jeri. Living across from me was an old man who also never left his room. He talked to himself and made scary grunting noises. A single woman in her 40s rented the last room down the hall, and she filled the one bathroom we all shared with enough cosmetic products to make the Kardashians jealous. She was always dashing out the door to go on her next hopeful date.

Now that I've set the scene, let me say, I'm a typical single-focus male. Once I'm into something, forget about getting my attention. I go all in. So I was deep into my theological studies, and I became a voracious reader. Life was simple. My biggest problem was trying to learn Greek grammar and vocabulary, and my second biggest problem was getting Jeri's damn notes about my late rent. I got those often. A minor oversight.

At this time, I also went to a midweek **Bible** study at my church. To teach the study, the church brought in John Courson, a well-known Bible teacher and pastor. Courson is a sizable man with a deep bellowing laugh. He's a gifted communicator who comes across as the father you never had but always wanted. Week after week, he packed out the church with several thousand people, more people than even the church's senior pastor could draw. Hundreds of people drove significant distances to hear Courson teach. Something about him drew the crowds.

I soon realized what that something was, and it annoyed me. Courson often talked to the crowd like they were hurting, suffering, and fearful. He ministered to the people as if everyone were broken. That annoyed my 23-year-old self. I thought, *Why does he always talk to us as if we're these poor hurting sheep, like we are victims and weak? What he needs to do—what he should do—is preach to us like we are soldiers and get us amped up for war. Man, they should let me up there. I'll whip these people into shape!*

Ah, the bliss of youthful arrogance.... I strutted around campus and through life with great confidence. Why wouldn't I? I knew almost everything there was to know! I knew where I was going in life, how it would look, and how I would get there. You see, the wheels of my life had not yet fallen off. Oh, I'd had a few slow leaks in life's tires, but nothing serious. I broke up with a girlfriend. That was tough. But let's be real: *I* broke up with *her*, and that's the easier side of a breakup. I also had to put up with Jeri and her strange house of circus oddities. I had to buy my own gas, clothes, and food. The struggle is real, right?

Now, almost 20 years since I heard him teach, I know why John Courson packed that church out. One hundred years ago, a pastor named Joseph Parker taught young seminary students, "Speak to the suffering, and you will never lack an audience. There is a broken heart in every crowd." Now I get it. The struggle for so many is real because life can be brutal at times. Courson spoke words of comfort and hope to people desperate for hope, for a way to make sense of all the pain, loss, anger, loneliness.... The list goes on. The point is, I'm in that crowd now. Maybe you are too. So, hope is humanity's universal language. We are hope-hungry creatures. But like 17-year-old me and 23-year-old me, we don't often think about hope... until the wheels of life fall off. But—as we will see—not all hopes are equal. Many things people put hope in will not and cannot deliver. Having these hopes is like a child playing with a rattlesnake: it seems fun and interesting at first... until it bites. Many hopes also bite when they're dashed and you're disappointed. Or crushed. So in this book I'm going to address real, true, and lasting hope, and I'm going to do it in a unique way I bet you've never seen before.

NO EASY ROAD

Fighting for hope is difficult, but that life-giving prize is absolutely worth the fight. In fact, finding and holding on to hope is necessary for life. Yet I know it's a lot easier to understand what I'll say about hope than it is to have that hope strongly rooted in your **heart** and then to live with hope when times get tough.

Before we go further, though, realize that hope comes in two steps. First is the big-picture hope, the conceptual. This learning about the nature of **reality** is the easier part of hope to grab onto. And this aspect is crucial. There is no hope without correct understanding and knowledge of ultimate reality. I'm talking about **worldviews**. If that's a new idea for you, don't worry, I'll explain more about this further on in the book. But this aspect—the Big picture—serves as the foundation and skeleton structure of your entire belief system.

The second step of hope is having and keeping that big picture securely in your heart. The challenge is—the fight is—to believe that hope is real and can be real for you specifically. Whenever we struggle and suffer—or when someone we love does—we can feel tempted to lose hope, lose **faith**, or get angry with God. **Truth** is the best weapon we have for this fight.

Let me also say that there is a world of difference between what *works* and what is *true*. Most people just want to find something that works for them, a quick fix, and immediate results. But we need to discover what is true because then hope will not only work, but it will work in the roughest storms and the darkest nights.

Finally, I've learned that there are no silver bullets, no simple solutions, and no easy steps to finding lasting hope. Life is not safe or predictable or easy. Life is hard, and some chapters are downright excruciating. I believe that another kind of hope works best for those situations. This kind of hope is big enough to change everything. It's what I call EPIC Hope.

PART **ONE**

WHYWE**HOPE**

CHAPTER 1

THE WHEELS FALL OFF

I TURNED 41 THIS year. It's wild how that happens. I feel like I was in high school only a few short years ago. And I'm still waiting for that day to arrive when I finally turn into a real adult. Like my parents.

Remember when you were a kid, around 10, and you looked at your parents or at your friend's parents, and you thought, *Now that's a full-blown adult!* That full-grown dad and full-on mom ran their own little kingdoms. (I could barely run my Sega video game system or keep a pet mouse alive!) They seemed to know everything, to have no fears, and to navigate life with complete confidence. My being one of those big ol' adults one day—that seemed a million miles away. Then I fall asleep, wake up, and I'm one of them! The only difference is, my kingdom stays together with duct tape, Band-Aids, alcohol, pain relievers, and ice cream. I know less now than I did in high school, I have a hundred more fears, and I am super thankful that my heart didn't go into cardiac arrest today.

THOSE HIGH-SCHOOL YEARS

When you think about it, high school can sort of jack you up....

It's like we all stand along a huge starting line with several hundred other kids our age. The gun fires, and all of us dash off in the race of life.

Now there are always those kids—you know the ones—who sort of fall by the wayside, the ones who fall asleep on the sidelines a few minutes after the gun fires, and the ones who wander off following butterflies. I love those kids because they eat my dust and make me feel good about myself.

But a lot of kids just kick butt, flip the switch, and blast like a rocket. I hate those kids. Goody-goodies. Know-it-alls. Kiss-ups. Nerds. And these kids become full-blown adults who master and command the sea of life… while I'm still trying to figure out how to fill out my stupid 1040 form. *Do I put a 1 or a 2 in that box?*

To this day, I still feel those kids' eyes. In my mind I still see them as teenagers, standing around "their" lunch tables. They're wearing stylish jean jackets, rocking their jock mullets, and holding binders full of finished homework and A papers. They watch me, size me up, and judge me. Just when I thought I was finally getting free from their influence, this thing called Facebook comes along. Son of a…

Thanks to technology, we can now spy on each other, compare scores, and see who's winning the race. Some classmates are still following butterflies. God bless them. My favorite, though, are the kick-ass kids who took off like a rocket but got lost, and now they also follow butterflies in far-off fields.

It hurts when I see on Facebook how old some of the people I graduated with look now—and then I realize that I'm the same age. God help me. That's when I need a lot of Netflix and a cigarette. *Wait, I quit smoking years ago. Crap. Okay, Netflix and some beers. Wait, I'm supposed to be a recovering alcoholic. Crap. Okay, Netflix, pizza, and ice cream. Okay, yeah, I can do that.* Yeah, high school sort of jacks you up.

IN SEARCH OF . . . GOD KNOWS WHAT

Earlier I just happened to mention in passing that minor thing about being a skinhead and having a big tattoo that says, "WHITE PRIDE." Not a big deal, right? Wanna skip it? Ugh, fine. You don't need to twist my arm. I'll spill—but I won't go into great depth because I've written about this elsewhere at length.[2] Here we go . . . .

One reason for the high school chaos is, I think, we're all desperately trying to figure out who we are. We try to find something—a style of music, a sport, a fashion, a cause, a religion, a sexual preference, a skill set, etc.—that gives us a sense of identity. Then we can say, "See *that*? *That's* what I'm all about." It's a way for us to feel like we belong somewhere. We also gain some bit of control and confidence. Hey! We're making sense of life!

But if you'd asked me then, "Who are you? What are you all about?" I would have stared at you. After some awkward silence, I might have mustered, "I don't know. I'm just me."

Anyway, people from different races attended my high school, and that made for some tension. So, since my friends and I were lost and confused about our own identity, we found an identity in being white. As immature men, we also felt weak and afraid of the world. Identifying as skinheads helped us feel powerful and strong. That's the same reason young people join gangs. We had no clue what life was about or who we were. It's that simple. Race was not the actual issue, although we thought it was.

So, you may be wondering, where were my parents in all this? I did this dangerous sport and broke bones, and I was a racist skinhead! What kind of parents did I *have*? I had good, loving parents who supported me in my sport even though it freaked them out. And the racism baffled and saddened them since they weren't like that. Around the age of 17, I became a real jerk. It was fueled by all

2 See my book *In Your Corner*, www.inyourcornerbook.com.

those feelings of being weak, afraid, and powerless. I masked that with anger and hate. And I put my sweet parents through hell.

During my senior year, I got into serious trouble with the law. In a single incident, I was charged with two felonies and a few misdemeanors. One charge was a hate crime. It's a long story, but the truth is, I was innocent. I didn't do what I was charged with, but my lawyer said the D.A. was out to set an example of the potential consequences of a hate crime. My parents hired an attorney who made a plea deal that kept me out of prison. But even that wasn't a wake-up call. I still didn't get it: I was rude and arrogant to the judge. I was just too dense to get it. Seriously.

I GOT MY BUTT KICKED . . . THANKFULLY

A couple years later I eased up on the tough guy stuff, grew out my hair, and stopped dressing like a thug. I took up golfing, enrolled in college, and tried to stay out of trouble. But I still loved to party and drink. For me, the purpose of life was to acquire money that would finance pleasure and fun. Life was all about partying and girls. What else was there?

When I was 19, a guy who was way cooler, way richer, and way tougher than I was confronted me. He was like the Total Man. He was everything I was not. His name was Jesus. He is also God incarnate. Minor detail. It didn't happen overnight, but I ended up surrendering my life to **Christ**. And Jesus kicked my butt.

He did it, first, with His absolute authority: He was God, and I was not. For me, Jesus wasn't about love initially. He knew that I needed to recognize who was in charge. You know, like *You betta recognize? Sucka.* That's what I needed. I'd always believed in God, and I thought He and I were cool because I wasn't *that* bad. Hey, plenty of people were far worse than me! But then I learned that's not how God—the one and only, the true and living God—measures things. With God, it's just Him and me. Gulp. "No, no, no! Don't look around to other people," God says. "You, Joel, you look to Me—and Me alone."

I wet myself a little. Okay, a lot.

After some time—and after changing my pants—I learned about God's great love and His truly amazing **grace**. I'll share more about that later, but what's important at this point of my story is this: I surrendered. I became a Christian.

And everything changed. And that change was much more profound than gaining a different identity. It was not at all like putting on a new shirt. Part of the everything was a huge paradigm shift. My new worldview had a revolutionary impact on me. I had discovered a coherent way to see all of reality—including myself and my purpose in life. For the first time ever, I realized that life had meaning. Life wasn't just a crapshoot I had to work out on my own and then pretend I'd found meaning.

I also noticed **creation** for the first time. I mean, I *really* noticed it: trees, flowers, clouds… I saw beauty. I'd never paid attention to that before. Suddenly, I saw the world as God's canvas that reflected His **infinite** creativity and splendor.

And my brain turned on! I started reading—a lot. I loved learning anything about anything. I also discovered a moral compass and a roadmap that showed me how a real man acts and loves.

Several years later, at 23, I went to seminary (that's school if you want to become a pastor). All I wanted to do was share with other people this news about the beauty and meaning I had discovered because Jesus kicked my butt. I also got a degree in **philosophy** from a local university. My passion—or specialty, if you will—is the more intellectual side of the Christian faith, the worldviews, **theology**, history, and philosophy. I'm a lot better at that stuff than I am at living the Christian life.

THE FIRST WHEELS FALL OFF

When I was 25, I was in love! She was 23, a new Christian, and a single mom of a three-year-old girl. We got married, I adopted her daughter, and suddenly I was a dad. I worked full-time while I was also a teaching pastor at a small church. Later I was an associate pastor at a church of about 500 people where I often taught and preached. I was also being invited to speak at other churches, conferences, and formal debates. We had a son together and moved into a big, brand-new house in Temecula, California. Look at me now, kick-ass kids from high school! I was checking off the right boxes on the ladder of success. Winning!

But that's the Facebook and Instagram snapshot. You know what I mean. Below the surface and behind closed doors were many foundational cracks—financial struggle, debt, unrealistic expectations, alcohol, verbal abuse, anger, and intimacy issues— that grew wider over time. Who's guilty of what is irrelevant at this point. It all existed on the back of the happy family photo.

After five years, she didn't love me anymore and wanted out. She added that she wanted a husband who made more money than I did. Deep knife wound. We did try marriage counseling a couple times, and although it helped for a while, it couldn't save the relationship. You see, saving a marriage requires that both parties *want* to make it work. Only one of us did; the other did not.

All this pain and drama occurred during the last two years of the marriage—and it was a terrible time. I desperately did not want to lose my family. I loved being a dad, and thoughts of not seeing my kids every day and my concern about how a divorce would harm them ripped me apart. I lived in constant pain and fear....

The first time I ever felt a need for hope was when I met Jesus. At that point, I knew I had no hope. I knew I was lost. The second time I needed hope was when I was walking through the pain-filled days at the end of my marriage. I often prayed and pleaded with God. Over the years I'd heard dozens of stories about God saving and renewing broken marriages, and I so wanted to be one of those stories. Besides, I'd given 10 years of my life to God, and I couldn't understand why He would allow everything to fall apart. I didn't lose my faith in God, but my faith definitely took a hit.

The divorce went through.

Shared custody.

Child support.

A broken family.

Broken me.

The wheels of life had fallen off. I had lost almost everything. The new house was gone. Most of the stuff we'd accumulated was gone. I lost getting to see my kids every day. I lost friends. I lost my job. I lost my reputation. I lost my desire to be a pastor. I often lost my desire to even live. On many occasions I *felt* utterly hopeless, but I didn't lose all hope because of certain things that I *knew*. Those things kept me going, though at times I was barely moving. But crawling is still moving! Those things I *knew* kept me from losing my faith. And it's those things that I'll share with you throughout this book. You see, certain things that I *know* make all the difference in my life. I want to share them so that you might know hope. Real hope.

TWO STEPS FORWARD, THREE STEPS BACK

The first year after the divorce, I was a wreck. I moved back into my dad's house, back into my old bedroom. That was depressing. I started smoking, and I drank a lot. Almost daily. I tried attending some get-togethers and birthday parties with friends, but seeing cheerful couples—especially those with kids—tore at my heart. I still went to church every Sunday, and I always took my kids with me. We had the weekends together, and I felt happiest then. I always tried to stay strong for them, and I always kept a cheery face. But my heart felt dead, like a zombie. Alcohol took away the pain, but it returned the next day... even heavier.

Around the second year after my divorce, I started working toward putting my life back together, however that would look. I started making smarter choices. Among them, I was reading—and I was reading a lot. I was reading less academic stuff on theology, philosophy, and **apologetics**. I focused more on books about the heart and our inner life, books written by therapists, counselors, and pastors. Much of Christianity had become like a sport: I knew the rules, I knew the players, and I knew the game, but my inner life dried in the process.

My effort to rebuild my life also included seeing a therapist for a while, joining Celebrate Recovery (the Christian version of AA), attending a divorce recovery group, going back to the gym, and starting to plug back in with friends. I felt closer to my kids more than ever. I also found a new job that I enjoyed.

Rebuilding takes time. It's not like starting with a clean slate or a wide-open field. Rebuilding is necessary when a structure has fallen. Of course, I had rubble to deal with as well as sharp glass, heavy beams, and some hidden skeletons. All that made my construction efforts more challenging, and I often felt I was taking two steps forward and three steps back. But I was committed to healing and starting over. By God's grace, I realized that the more of myself I gave to Him, the more the rubble cleared, and the more progress I made on my rebuilding project.

By the third year, I was feeling like a new man. It was as if I'd had a terrible car wreck, as if my car had slammed into a tree known as reality. The impact sent me through the windshield and sliding across rock-strewn ground. But I got up, looked around, evaluated the situation, and learned a ton of life lessons from it all. In fact, I actually got to the point where I was genuinely thankful for all the mess. I also clearly saw how sick and broken that marriage relationship had been. So, yes, I was thankful. I could thank God for that wreck and everything that I learned from it.

Now, I'd always told myself that I wouldn't even think about dating for at least one year after the divorce. Well, one year turned into three years. I had more rubble and junk to deal with than I'd expected. But I wanted to heal the right way. And I definitely did not want to walk into any new relationship with a limp.

Yet while I was going through my divorce and dealing with my brokenness, a young woman in Oregon was going through her own tragedy and experiencing her own brokenness. Rebekah was 23 when stage 1 breast cancer invaded her life. But let's back up. I'll let her tell her story.

CHAPTER 2

THE GIRL FROM OREGON

REBEKAH

WELL, I WAS born in southern Oregon. I am fourth in the lineup of five siblings. Although there is an age gap of twenty years between my oldest brother and younger sister, we all share the same parents.

My biological dad was an alcoholic suffering from untreated schizophrenia. He physically and verbally abused my mom, and when I was three years old, my parents divorced. My mom, my siblings, and I moved to the Bay Area in California.

Mom got remarried when I was around seven years old. His name was Dave, and I called him *Dad*. He was a loving dad, but he, too, suffered from his own problems. He also abused my mom physically... and me, verbally.

My childhood wasn't always easy, but it wasn't terrible either. My mom became a Christian in the early '80s and raised the three youngest of us five in the church. Mom also sent us to a private Christian school until my freshman year of high school.

One morning when I was twelve, my mom got a call from the hospital regarding my biological dad. Someone had found him unconscious under an overpass, and paramedics had taken him to the hospital. Because of the stage of his illness, he had never received any help or treatment, and he had spent the past few years homeless. When we visited him at the hospital, I was hoping to get him back... only to find out that all his organs were failing. Three days later he passed away from cirrhosis of the liver. I had a special place in my heart for my dad. I had always longed for him to come back and be my dad. When he died, it was like a permanent hole opened up in my heart.

After my freshman year of high school, we moved back to Oregon—without my stepdad. I spent my last three years of high school at a large public school. In the Bay Area, I had known many people at my little private school, but in Oregon I was lonely, depressed, and friendless. Yet I had always gone to youth group at church, and I continued. My faith really came alive during that time. I clung to the only father who had stayed constant throughout my life: my heavenly Father.

After making it through high school, I planned to go to Biola University to study nursing. I got accepted there and took the entrance exams for the RN program. I had always dreamed of being a nurse in an **oncology** unit: I wanted to help people with cancer. But through a series of unexpected circumstances, the door to Biola closed. I had a powerful sense that God was telling me that it wasn't time for college and that He had something else for me.

I spent the next few years out of the country, serving the Lord. I spent almost a year at an orphanage in Baja serving disabled kids and adults. It was very humbling. Then I moved to Mazatlán where I worked for a missionary family as a homeschool teacher to their children. After that, I spent a year in Europe as an *au pair* (nanny) for two families, one in Germany and the other in Ireland. After that, I knew it was time to get back home and spend time with my family.

When I got out of the shower one day, I looked in the mirror and noticed an odd bruise over my right breast. When I felt it, I found a lump. I was 23 and didn't think breast cancer was possible at such a young age. But I looked it up on Dr. Google to see what he thought, and there I read that only 1 in 100,000 women under the age of 25 are at risk of getting breast cancer. To be safe, I made an appointment to have some tests done.

Waiting for those results made for the longest weekend of my life. When the phone call came, it was just like in the movies: "Miss Ruby [my maiden name], can you come in as soon as possible? And we advise you to bring someone with you." I had stage 1 breast cancer. My heart sank, and a whole host of new fears entered my life. As Joel says, the wheels of life had fallen off. Yet a few days later when I started a journal, this was the first thing I wrote: "God, I know that You are good, and I know that You are faithful and that You have a plan even if I can't see it right now."

After three medical opinions, I decided to have a double mastectomy. All three doctors said it would give me the best chance to keep the cancer from ever coming back. It was a grueling decision and even more difficult to see myself in the mirror after surgery. Soon afterward, though, I met with a plastic surgeon who did reconstructive surgery.

My first day of chemotherapy, I walked through the front door of the oncology clinic and started laughing. I'd always imagined myself working as a nurse in an oncology unit, not a patient! I spent six months doing chemo, followed by biological and hormone therapy. After a year, tests showed I was cancer-free.

Soon after that, I learned one reason why God had allowed me to walk through that painful chapter. Part of my treatment required routine echocardiograms, which is a fancy way doctors can get a 3D look at your heart. On that visit, the tech looked at my heart in a place no previous doctor had ever looked.

Minutes later the doctor came in. They had discovered two sizeable holes in my atrium that restricted blood from circulating through my organs. Apparently, I had been experiencing minor episodes of heart failure for a while, but thinking it was a side-effect of the chemo, I'd shrugged it off. The doctor told me that, had they not caught it, within months I would have either had a stroke or simply passed away in my sleep. I had open heart surgery, and they repaired my heart. In the oddest way, cancer had saved my life!

Having cancer changed me. I learned so much about what really matters in life. And, just as Joel had done, I had to start the rebuilding process. It all had happened so fast—the news of cancer, all the doctors, the treatments, the surgery, etc.—it was as if I was on autopilot. I didn't have time to process all the emotions prompted by what was happening. So, after all my treatments, I struggled with PTSD, but I didn't realize it. I just knew that I was messed up inside. A great therapist helped me see the PTSD for what it was and gave me tools to work through it.

Cancer had put my life on hold. A few months after my heart surgery, I heard that faint whisper that said I was due for a new adventure. It was time for me to learn to start living again. My younger sister lived in Southern California with her family, and

I felt a tug in my heart to head down there. I packed up my little car and drove down to sunny Southern California.

WHEELS BACK ON, WHEELS BACK OFF

Well, Rebekah and I ended up finding each other. We met online on a site for Christian singles. She was 26, and I was 36. Yep, I scored. We talked a lot, and a deep love for one another took root.

We both agree that our hard experiences broke us, changed us in positive ways, and actually prepared us for each other. We also agree that, had we not gone through those dark chapters, we probably wouldn't fit together so well, if at all. Also, those dark chapters prepared us for the even darker chapters that waited for us soon after we married.

In 2014, we were married up in Rebekah's hometown, Ashland, Oregon. But I needed to live close to my kids, so we moved into a little apartment back in Orange County, California. Since I shared custody of my kids, Rebekah and I had our home all to our newlywed selves a good portion of the time. Yep, I scored.

Six months into our marriage, my dad called me one day.

"Hey, buddy! How ya doing?"

"Hey, Dad! I'm good. What's up?"

"Well, I don't want you to worry, but I've been seeing the doctor and doing some tests."

"Okay, what's going on?"

"Well, they found something in me that's not so good. But it's still early, and I don't want you to worry. I'll be fine."

"Dad! What the heck are you talking about?"

"They found some cancer in me—but we still have more tests to do."

Cancer? What the . . . I didn't even know what cancer was except that it was freaky bad. My dad looked and seemed healthy. He had just retired and had many plans for this new chapter of his life.

Cancer? My dad was like my North Star on earth. He was always there for me. When my life fell apart, he took me back in. He saw me at my worst and loved me through it. He—and my mom—never gave up on me.

We later found out that my dad had stage 4 stomach cancer. There's no stage 5, if you know what I mean. Stage 4 means that the cancer has spread or metastasized to other organs or places in the body. Most stage 4 cancers are incurable. The goal is to fight as much of it as you can and manage it for as long as you can until it takes over.

Two months later, Rebekah, at 27, was re-diagnosed with stage 4 breast cancer.

All four wheels of life fell off… again.

The spare tire vanished.

And the engine froze up.

But let's back up a bit….

Eight months into our marriage, Rebekah started getting bad back pain, but she thought it was because she was standing on her feet all day at work. One morning, her back hurt so much that she could barely get out of bed. I decided we needed to get her to the ER to figure out what was going on. At the hospital, they did a CT scan of her body. We waited and joked around in the little hospital room… until a sober-faced doctor came in with papers.

"Mrs. Hughes, we found masses in your kidney and lungs. Given your history, I think you need to see your oncologist [cancer doctor] right away."

What? No! No…. No…. Our hearts sank, and deep fear took a white-knuckle grip on us. I felt it physically in my chest and my throat. *No. No. No!*

When tragedy strikes—when all four wheels of life fall off in one instant—a desperate hope emerges, a hope that is fueled at least in part by denial. It can soften the blow and keep us from completely dissolving into **despair**. Driving home from the ER that night, Rebekah and I were both somber, weighed down by the heavy news, but we held on to the desperate hope that these masses were just benign cysts. They could be. They *have* to be. *God, please...*

The next day we packed some bags and drove straight up to Oregon to see Rebekah's oncologist. They did a battery of tests on her: a CAT scan, an MRI, blood work, and a biopsy. It took several days for the results, and waiting was awful. Finally, we got a call to come in. Rebekah's oncologist walked in and sat down. We both knew instantly from his face.

"Mrs. Ruby [he had known her when she was single], I'm sorry, but the cancer is back. The tests revealed that it has spread to your kidneys, lungs, liver, and hip bone. We also found at least nine tumors in your brain. I'm so sorry...."

As hard as I try, even now I cannot put into words the feelings of that moment. My emotions imploded. Fear. Terror. Sadness. Sorrow. Anger. Rage. Panic. Resistance. Pain. In a single instant, all of this—and more—was rolled up in a single ball in my heart. BOOM! Tears fell.... All three of us were crying.

"What does this mean? Is this stage 4?" Rebekah asked.

"Yes, I'm sorry. You have stage 4 breast cancer."

The next day we met with a different oncologist. After reviewing her scans, he said that her cancer was so advanced that she probably had about four to six months of life—and even that would require treatment. That night I called my dad to tell him. Remember, he too was battling stage 4 cancer. He broke down in tears. *F-ing cancer....*

Before we met, Rebekah and I had both experienced pain and loss that resulted in our brokenness, confusion, and fear. It was as if the lenses of the binoculars through which we were looking at life clouded up, and the future blurred. After we—individually and together—spent some years rebuilding, the pieces of life had come back together, but in new ways, better ways. By the time we got married, we could clearly see a wonderful future. We were excited. We had dreams and plans. There was a possibility of a child or children (gulp). But the moment the oncologist said, "The cancer is back," the lens caps shuttered the binoculars. The future went black.

FIGHTING FOR HOPE

My dad's doctors expected him to live about a year. He did a couple rounds of brain radiation, but then he stopped. My sister and I encouraged him to keep fighting, to start chemotherapy, but he said no. He didn't want to go through that. He was 69 years old, still young, but he told me he'd lived an enjoyable life and had no regrets. We didn't understand it, but the choice was ultimately his. Looking back, I think he didn't want to eat up all his savings to stave off the inevitable. I think he wanted to leave an inheritance to my sister and me. He wanted to help us. He was choosing to die early in order to help secure our future. He was doing what he did best: he was being a dad.

Rebekah, however, chose to fight. She rallied with faith and hope before I did. The City of Hope cancer center in Duarte, California (a suburb of Los Angeles), accepted her case, and God blessed Rebekah with an amazing oncologist. Dr. Lucille Leong (and later Dr. James Waisman) consulted with renowned specialists around the country concerning Rebekah's case, and they devised the best plan of attack. Dr. Leong radiated hope, and we felt like we could breathe again. (As I write this, I'm surprised to realize that was almost five years ago!) The City of Hope has beaten most of Rebekah's cancer, and she's in what is called *"near* complete remission." She's not healed, but she's doing well. *Thank You, thank You, Lord.*

About a year after receiving the diagnosis, we started a company called Rebekah's Hope (https://www.rebekahshope.org/) that "exists to equip those fighting cancer, illness, and despair, find hope and healing through our writings, movie, and e-courses." We partnered with a talented filmmaker and made a feature documentary called *A Brave Hope* about Rebekah's journey. I published two books dealing with cancer care. Rebekah is also writing a book about her journey and what she's learned along the way. We created "The HOPE Project," an online course for individuals fighting cancer and cancer support groups. And all of this was possible because of the inheritance my dad left me.

My dad's choice reminds me of something Jesus said once: *"Unless a kernel of wheat falls to the ground and dies, it remains only a single seed. But if it dies, it produces many seeds"* (John 12:24). My dad was just one man, small in stature, insignificant and unknown to the world, but because of his loving sacrifice, many thousands will find blessings and hope.

Well, there you have it: my credentials for writing about hope. I've known deep brokenness, depression, dread, anger, and despair—many times. I've also known deep joy, hope, and love—more times. Hope—genuine, **objective** HOPE—has saved me many times. It still does. I'm here today and Rebekah is here today because of certain things we know about hope, things we'll get to later in this book.

But first, we need to further explore the idea of hope. In the next chapter, we'll see how crucial hope is to our lives—literally. But that's not enough. It's not enough to know that we all need hope; we also need to know what the heck we're talking about when we use the word *hope*. We will look at the concept of hope in chapter 4.

Did you remember to bring your scuba tank? You forgot yours? No worries. I have an extra one you can borrow. You'll need it because, together, we're going to dive deeper and deeper.

CHAPTER 3

THE NECESSITY OF HOPE

ONE OF REBEKAH's and my favorite things to do is "go to our place." I say, "I can't wait to get to our place," and she responds, "Yes, the place where we belong." We go to our place at the end of a long day, when we need it and we feel like we've earned it. We get everything ready: we prop up pillows, turn on the fan, open the laptop to either Netflix or Prime, and put dinner or a treat on each bedside table. Our favorite place is bed!

Like most of us nowadays, we have our favorite shows. One amazing series we enjoyed on Amazon Prime is called *I Shouldn't Be Alive*. Every episode is a nail-biting story of some person or group of people who get caught in situations they should not have survived, but by some miracle, they do. People get stuck in the middle of a desert or a jungle or a mountain or an ocean. They're out there for days without food or water or shelter, often hurt and lost. It's the middle of the third season right now, and we've probably seen close to 30 incredible stories.

I've noticed a pattern in these accounts that are told by the actual survivors. In almost every story, the person or people are in their predicament for days, and they take viewers right up to the point when they are about to die. Sometimes they are only minutes from dying. In almost every case, after fighting long and hard to survive, after doing all they could to hold onto the hope that they'll get rescued, they reach the point where they physically and mentally can go no further. They are 100 percent done. They collapse. They give up. They are ready to let death win.

But—and this is the pattern—something happens, and they are rescued. Sometimes a stranger appears, a plane or helicopter spots them, the storm lets up, or they notice exactly what they need. Every time, at that moment, hope bursts forth. These people instantly find new power, new energy, and a new ability to get up and keep moving until they get rescued.

In most episodes, just when all hope seems lost, these survivors accept that their death is imminent and simply give up. But the moment hope breaks in, they find mental and even physical renewal.

THE DIFFERENCE BETWEEN LIFE AND DEATH

In each of those survival stories, one thing—the same thing in every case—made the difference between life and death. That one thing was... hope.

Next to faith and love, hope is one of the most powerful forces in the universe. In fact, hope is crucial to life itself. Hope is on par with oxygen, water, and food. You won't die as fast with a loss of hope as you would with a loss of air, water, or food, but a person who lives with a sustained absence of hope will perish soon enough.

Over the years I've had a number of friends commit suicide. The loss is heart-wrenching and destructive to the family and friends of these people. This kind of death is not the same as someone who gets killed in a car accident or dies because of a health-related issue. Suicide is sinister in the way it leaves loved ones with so many unanswered questions, so much guilt, and—worst, of all—so many "If I had only…" thoughts. Suicide is actually a terribly selfish act although it doesn't feel that way to the person who makes that choice. I get that.

When I was 24, a friend shot himself in the head with a shotgun. Another friend found him in his room on his queen-size bed. Scattered around him: the divorce papers from his wife.

At 30, a friend overdosed in a motel room, pushed to that point by his extended unemployment. The note he left revealed a man who had lost all hope of ever providing for his family.

At 40, a friend who, on the outside, was a picture of complete success, but for years he battled fierce demons on the inside. He drove his car full-speed into a wall.

And all of us are familiar with celebrities who have taken their own lives. Ernest Hemingway, Marilyn Monroe, Kurt Cobain, Robin Williams, Kate Spade, Chester Bennington, and Anthony Bourdain are some of these people who appeared to have it all, who appeared to be leading lives that most of us only dream of, yet something was missing, something powerful enough to tempt them to want to die.

I never contemplated suicide until the first time all the wheels of life fell off. Before that, whenever I felt sad or experienced heartbreak, I always told myself that I'd get through it somehow: *Hang in there, man. You'll make it through.* I didn't understand why my friend killed himself just because he was going through a divorce. But I was naïve: *It's only a divorce. It's not the end of the world. Buck up, buddy. There's more fish in the sea! Get back up on that horse.* Blah, blah, blah.

But then *I* went through a divorce—and you don't "just go through" a divorce! Granted, not everyone feels torn apart, but for many people, divorce is like having your heart and soul go through a tree shredder. A massive part of your identity gets shredded, your purpose for working gets shredded, your routine and lifestyle get shredded, your family gets shredded, your kids get shredded, and even your physiological chemical stability gets shredded. And, for many people, their faith in God gets shredded.

There I was. Alone in a dingy motel room. Lying on a crusty queen-size bed. I didn't have a gun (my close friend had wisely taken my handgun to his house), but I did have alcohol. *A lot* of alcohol. After four days in that room, eating no food, drinking no water, and consuming only massive amounts of alcohol, I was severely dehydrated and close to death. My breathing was short and slow. Cigarette smoke fogged the room. I figured I would fall asleep and not wake up. Tears falling, I scrawled a goodbye note to my kids telling them how much I loved them and that I was sorry.

I didn't want to die, but I also didn't see even a flicker of light in this darkness. I didn't see how life could ever get better. I definitely didn't see my God hearing, much less answering, my desperate cries and prayers. Rationality and perspective are often early casualties of pain and suffering. From the outside, we can look at such a person's life and see so much good and a lot of real potential, but when we ourselves are in that place, we can't see it—or even if we can see some good and a little potential, we don't believe it. At that point, I didn't see any reason to go on— and even if I had, I wouldn't have believed it was legitimate. I was broken. I was lost....

I'm writing this chapter in an airplane 40,000 feet in the air. Rebekah, her mom, and I are flying to New York. For the last two years we've worked our butts off filming *A Brave Hope*, a documentary about Rebekah's life and her journey with cancer. Our film is a semifinalist in a film festival, and we hope to win and land a distribution deal. Even though we still have many serious trials in our life—like Rebekah's stage 4 cancer and my sporadic desire to drink—our lives are rich, full of purpose, and far better than I could have imagined. Why the difference between me in that motel room and me on this plane? Hope. I'm on this plane because of hope. I'm alive today because of hope. And I left that motel room, barely, because of a faint hope, but hope nevertheless. (BTW, we're back home now, winners of the Best Documentary award.)

GENERATION ANGST: IN NEED OF HOPE

We could describe our current cultural climate with many words: *innovative, tolerant, narcissistic, impatient, lazy, isolated, cooperative*.... Everyone's list will look different. One word I think I would find on nearly every list is angst.

Angst is that deep, underlying, unsettling, restless feeling that something is wrong—and that something will get worse, not better. This kind of anxiety is a painful sense of **existential** incompleteness and emptiness. Angst vibrates in our souls because of that one thing—whatever it is—that's missing because that one thing feels like everything. New things, new experiences, new people, new goals, or new drugs—none of these settle the angst, but we keep trying. We don't know what else to do. We need hope.

We are the most depressed, anxious, and drugged generation in the world's history. Shareholders and executives at the big pharmaceutical companies secretly love the growth of angst in our world. Now, I'm not against antidepressants or other mood-stabilizing drugs for people who need them, either for life or for a season, but we all know—and research shows—we as a culture are way over-drugged. We need hope.

We are the most high and most drunk generation in the

world's history. For 40 years, we've been fighting the war against drugs to no avail. Decades ago, the monster was cocaine; today, speed—or crystal meth—overruns many cities and states. As a nation, we are also experiencing an opioid epidemic: opioid overdoses now claim more lives annually than breast cancer does and more lives than car accidents do.[3] We need hope.

And medical marijuana is knocking down walls of prohibition in state after state like a row of *Dominoes*. In Orange County (where I live) and Los Angeles County (next door) are dozens, if not several hundred, pot shops. You can get a "medical" prescription for any perceived or professed condition. My friend's 18-year-old son got one because he feels nervous sometimes. In reality, he's the one who buys for his buddies, and they all get high together in the backyard. Where I live, pot and CBD oil are advertised on freeway billboards, radio stations, and sign spinners on street corners.

I'm not going to pontificate about the goodness or badness of smoking pot or using CBD oil. Rebekah uses CBD oil every once in a while for legitimate medical purposes. And, yes, she gets a bit loopy sometimes, but not on purpose. I bring up drugs, whether legal or illegal, only to make the point that something is changing on a grand scale: we 21st-century human beings can no longer face everyday reality. Or maybe we don't want to. Something about reality is too painful, too terrifying, too boring, too overwhelming, even too depressing. Not knowing what to do about it, we—naturally—seek to escape it. We medicate it with mind- and body-numbing pleasure, entertainment, or substances—or all three combined. We need hope.

We choose constant distraction rather than engaged, conscious

---

3 https://www.campusdrugprevention.gov/news/opioids-now-kill-more-people-breast-cancer and https://www.benefitspro.com/2019/01/18/opioids-now-kill-more-people-than-cars-do/?slreturn=20190816085547

interaction with loved ones, friends, and even work, and I think most of us do this because we don't know what to do with ourselves. Boredom and silence are among our greatest enemies. Acting as mirrors of reality, they reveal our inner emptiness and insignificance. We are an anxious generation. The world—our worlds—are moving at breakneck speed, and we simply can't keep up. We feel overwhelmed and fearful about the future. If you can relate to any of this, know that I'm right there too.

So, what do we do? Is there any hope of finding hope? Where can we find a hope strong enough to give us the courage we desperately need to face both ourselves and a vast, unknown future? I think there is hope for us still, but first we need to know more precisely what we're talking about. As a philosopher, I'm keen on defining our terms. Since *hope* is our key term, let's look more closely at what we're talking about because we tend to use that word in many ways.

CHAPTER 4

THE NATURE OF HOPE

I F YOU WATCH our documentary, *A Brave Hope*, Rebekah's faith, courage, and character—in the face of stage 4 cancer—will inspire you. The film took two years to create. It was a lot more work than I ever expected....

One important task in writing a book or making a movie is deciding on a title. What do we call it? A lot of thought and strategizing goes into choosing a title. It's a make-or-break thing: you only have one chance at a first impression! We filtered through dozens of ideas—and landed on *A Brave Hope*. Bam! That was it. Those three simple words powerfully encapsulated everything the film is about, and they meant something special to Rebekah and me.

"BUT I'M BRAVE!"

Rebekah often says to me, "But I'm brave." Yet when she does, she says it in a little girl voice and a joking manner. For example, both of us are introverts and can feel intimidated by public social events. I'll say to her before we go in, "Are you ready for this?" She responds with "Yes. Remember, I'm brave."

But—and this is interesting—Rebekah is actually not very brave about many things. She's actually a big scaredy-cat about so much in life. She's afraid of the dark. She can't be in a different room without me if it's dark. She will run to me to get away from the dark.

We can't watch scary movies. (I lost that whole genre when we got married.) Even the covers scare her. When we've been looking at the Redbox selections at the grocery store and a scary movie cover appears, she's actually slapped her hand against it to cover it. Whatever the image was, it scared her!

So—and this won't surprise you—in the world of Hughes, it's absolutely against the law for me to scare her. No jumping out and giving her a quick fright. No telling a scary story. I've gotten in big trouble for doing both those things. To this lawbreaker, it's funny; to her, it's frightening. She's also afraid of public social situations, of personal confrontation, and of most bugs—especially cockroaches (she calls them *las cucarachas*).

Now, most of us aren't really afraid of scary movies or cockroaches. When we were kids, we may have been fearful of the dark, but most of us outgrew such fears. But you know what does terrify us? Do you know what fills our hearts with dread? The "C" word. *Cancer.*

And here is another interesting fact: in her battle against cancer, terminal cancer, *her* cancer, Rebekah is remarkably brave. Oh, she's human and has occasional moments of fear, but she is braver than most. She's much braver than I would be.

WHAT IS IT?

Here's the million-dollar question: how? How can Rebekah be so brave? What makes this ordinary, shy girl so brave? What is the source of her courageous hope in the face of death? What gave me hope enough to pull myself out of a dark motel and out of an even darker mindset? What gives both of us a courageous hope and strength to stay in this fight? That's what people want to know. That's what people *need* to know. What's the secret sauce?

Well—as promised earlier—let's look more closely at hope. What is *hope*? Well, we use the word *hope* for everything just like we use the word *love*: I love pepperoni pizza with a side of Ranch dressing. That's my favorite food in the whole wide world. I love it! I love books and writing. I love *The Office, The Walking Dead,* and *The Lord of the Rings.* I love creativity. I love my kids. I love my wife.

We use the word *hope* in the same broad way: I hope the pizza gets here soon. I hope I get into that school. I hope I meet the deadline. I hope the neighbors are quiet tonight because I'd like to sleep. I hope my team gets to the Super Bowl. I hope the kids have fun. I hope Rebekah knows how much I love her. But are any of these the kind of hope that keeps Rebekah battling cancer?

To better understand hope, let's first look at its opposite: despair, also known as hopelessness. Despair is that deep feeling and solid belief that your condition will never improve, your situation cannot be resolved, and no way out of your current problems even exists. Despair is the idea and belief that circumstances will never get better and there's no point in trying. When we are hopeless, we give up the fight; we concede defeat.

Clearly, like hope, despair is more than a feeling. For sure, the feelings are there, and they are strong. In fact, when we are in those times of despair, we *feel* like despair is the only reality: the *feeling* of pain and despair can be all-consuming. And because that feeling is so strong, despair has real power—but it's not the kind of power we want. It's a sinister power that bears down on us, pushing us closer and closer to the ground, and if we don't find the strength to stop it, we'll be buried.

MORE THAN A FEELING

The powerful feelings of pain, fear, and despair blind us to a deeper reality: hopelessness is more than a feeling. Hopelessness is a *mindset* or a *belief* that we hold on to.

In the same way, hope is a *mindset* or a *belief* that we hold on to. Sure, hope is a feeling that has great power, a bright and beautiful power, the kind of life-giving power we want. True hope—EPIC Hope—creates within us an emotional reservoir of power that enables us to push onward. But hope is more than a feeling of empowerment. That feeling is a fruit of hope, of your choice to hold on to the belief that you will make it, that relief or rescue will come.

Yet such beliefs and mindsets don't exist in isolation. Neither do they just come to you from nowhere in a *Eureka!* moment. Hope and despair—these two beliefs about your circumstances and your future—depend on *other beliefs* that are woven into a web of beliefs called your worldview.

Simply put, your worldview is the unique way that you see the world. It's how you interpret events and try to make sense out of reality. A worldview is a network of **presuppositions** about what reality is, about how we know things, and about how we ought to behave. Presuppositions are like assumptions, but they go deeper. Basically, these presuppositions are our ultimate core beliefs lodged deep in our subconscious.

Think of your worldview like a spider's web, each strand representing a belief you hold. On the outskirts of the web are beliefs that you hold loosely. Revising or even abandoning these beliefs wouldn't distress you much. *I think it will rain tomorrow, but it might not. I believe that this is a good computer and will last me another four or five years, but if not, it won't kill me. I believe I'll be safe eating Taco Bell this late at night, but I could be wrong... painfully wrong.*

You get the idea.

As we move closer to the center of the web, however, our hold on those beliefs becomes stronger until we reach our central beliefs, those that are highly resistant to revision as well as our nonnegotiables. These core beliefs are our presuppositions that serve as the foundation for our outlook on life, for our worldview. What we think, what we say, what we say we "know," and what we believe to be right and wrong—all stem from these inner core beliefs, many which we're not even aware we have. Many people pick up their beliefs like a dog picks up fleas. The dog's got 'em, for sure, but if you ask her where she got them, she'll cock her head and stare at you. She ain't got a clue, but she knows she's got 'em.

Ultimately, each of us holds our worldview by faith, not because of scientific proof, sense experience, or popular opinion. But not every worldview provides hope, let alone a powerful hope. By their nature, many worldviews and philosophies instead foster doubt, despair, and therefore hopelessness. For many people, finding new hope begins with recognizing the harmful or false beliefs at their core, rejecting those beliefs, and then adopting new beliefs that will generate hope.

POWER GENERATORS

While hope and hopelessness are more than feelings, they are also not just sterile philosophical beliefs. We are not robots. We are complex, often emotion-driven beings. (I like to see us as beautiful messes.) *The degree and the kind of hope or hopelessness we have begins with, rests on, and stems from our* ultimate beliefs. Our beliefs—particularly our core beliefs—bring forth the fruit of hope, despair, or some combination of the two.

This fruit is the emotional aspect of hope and despair: we *feel* hopeful, or we *feel* hopeless, and both act as reservoirs of emotional power and strength. It sounds weird to think of despair as a power. But feelings of despair definitely have the power to push us in a certain direction, and that direction would be down. The power of despair leaves us immobilized. Isolated. Stuck. Desperate. Terrified. Depressed. Done.

Likewise, finding hope—the right kind of hope (more on this to come!)—has the opposite effect. True hope gives rise to feelings characterized by a power that leads us in a certain direction, and that direction would be up. The power of hope enables us to feel freed. Empowered. Confident. Encouraged. Energetic. Moving.

One problem that we all face—one trap we all fall into—is following the *feelings* without addressing our underlying *beliefs*. We do this because going with our feelings is a lot easier than figuring out this worldview stuff. Watching a YouTube video or Googling a brief article about changing our surface thoughts and feelings would be much easier and quicker than thinking through our core beliefs and trying to figure out what we think reality is or considering the ultimate meaning of life. You know, all that crazy kind of stuff that philosophers like. Besides, no one already bordering on hopeless feelings has the energy or desire to do all that.

Even before social media hit, we human beings have loved quick fixes and easy cures. I'm no different. Some of those efforts—like reciting mantras or practicing positive thinking—may help, but they rarely work for long. Fighting hopelessness and finding hope is like everything else in life: you get out what you put in. When we lazily seek simple solutions, we get, well, weak and short-lived results.

But don't worry. I've spent the last 20 years studying all this, and I'll do most of the heavy lifting for you. Most of it. I do ask one thing from you: whoever you are and wherever you're at, I ask you to not give up. I ask you to muster a bit of faith and trust me. I want some fresh hope to sprout in you, and I do believe that our journey together may change everything for you. Yes, we will continue to dive more deeply into these waters, but I've dived in them many times. Stay close and you'll be fine. I know where I'm going, and I can't wait to show you.

In the next chapter, we'll continue to look at the nature of hope, and I will shed a lot of light on this very ambiguous word.

CHAPTER 5

THE LEVELS OF HOPE

B EFORE I STARTED writing this book, the concept of hope had dominated my thoughts for months. The more I thought about hope, the more I started realizing that different kinds of hope exist. And of course hopes differ because needs differ. The more we have at stake to lose, the more important hope becomes to us. Seems obvious, but I never thought about hope like that until, well, until I consciously started thinking about it. Go figure.

LEVELS OF HOPE

As I thought about what hope is, I saw ways to categorize these different kinds of hope based on the weight of what's at stake and the severity of the consequences should what we hope for not materialize. I came to the conclusion that hope comes in three levels: Mundane, Moderate, and Mega. Let's look at some examples.

1. *MUNDANE HOPES* are exactly what you think. These hopes may or may not come to pass, but it's not a big deal either way. Of course, life is not always this simple. Behind-the-scenes issues in a person's life can suddenly or gradually make a

seemingly Mundane issue into a Moderate or even a Mega issue. Here are some examples of everyday Mundane hopes:

- You hope that your casserole turns out well. You've made it a dozen times without fail, but you never know.

- You hope that you pass your math test tomorrow. You've studied all you can, and you always do fine on your tests, but you never know.

- You hope that your team wins an important game. They're favored, but you never know.

What can we say about these Mundane hopes? First, these outcomes may or may not happen, but the stakes are typically low unless, of course, you do something really stupid like bet your life savings and your house on the big game. But under normal conditions, if these events you hope for don't come to pass, you shrug your shoulders and say, "Next time."

Second, more often than Moderate or Mega hopes do, Mundane hopes tend to stem from previous experiences. What do I mean? Look back at the three examples. In each case, we've tried, practiced, and succeeded before. We don't know the future, but based on our past experience, we are relatively confident that there will be a success again. We call this inductive reasoning (we come to a conclusion based on specific events in the past), and even though we are unaware of the process as it unfolds in our minds, it comprises most of our thinking.

Since Mundane hopes are connected to past experience, the results are usually highly predictable, and we can be fairly confident about the outcome, good or bad. Yet each example I gave ended with "But you never know." That's true because we rarely know the future with absolute certainty, but most of the time we can be confident about what the outcome will be. When we can be fairly confident, though, are our thoughts and feelings actually hopes? Sort of, but they're pretty mundane. In talking about them, in fact, we may actually be using the word *hope* colloquially rather than literally. At this level, we aren't speaking about a heartfelt hope we want and *need* to happen.

Third, let me ask you this: Is a Mundane hope unique to people of a certain age? No. Does a person's race matter? No. How about that individual's worldview or religion? Nope. It doesn't matter if the person is an agnostic, a Hindu, a Christian, a Muslim, an atheist, or a dude on the couch smoking weed and hoping that bag of Doritos is still in the cupboard. Everyone has Mundane hopes.

Let's take it up a notch.

2. **MODERATE HOPES** are weightier than Mundane, but for most people, their world doesn't come crashing down if their Moderate hopes don't come to pass. Here are some examples:

- You *really* hope that you get this new job. That would change your life big-time.

- You *really* hope that you don't get fired from your job. That would change your life big-time.

- You *really* hope that you find a solution so the bank doesn't take your house. That would change your life big-time.

As you can see, these hopes are on a different level than Mundane hopes. Moderate hopes are a much bigger deal: whatever happens *would definitely change your life* for better or worse. Because of this level of importance, we really want these hopes to materialize: we want to be hired, we don't want to be fired, and we want to find the money. Moderate hopes like these wake us up to the value of **prayer**.

Also, did you notice that Moderate hopes are accompanied by far less confidence and certainty than Mundane hopes? One reason is, we don't usually have any experience with the circumstances that prompt Moderate hopes. We can't look at the past for clues about what might happen in the future. Moderate hopes are, therefore, closer to what we usually think of when we talk about hope. With Mundane hopes, we have a significant degree of control over the outcomes, but with Moderate hopes, we often have little to no control. We are less confident and more vulnerable.

Again, let me ask you this. Is a Moderate hope unique to people of a certain age? No. Does a person's race matter? No. How about that individual's worldview or religion? Nope. It doesn't matter if the person is an agnostic, a Hindu, a Christian, a Muslim, an atheist, or a dude on the couch smoking weed and hoping that the cop car that pulls up outside isn't there for him. Everyone has Moderate hopes.

Let's notch this up again.

3. **MEGA HOPES** are, yes, Mega. Huge. Determinative. Often irreversible. Mega hopes almost always deal with life-and-death matters or at least severe life-altering circumstances. Mundane hopes are basically inconsequential, and we can usually shrug off even a negative outcome. Moderate hopes are more significant, introducing an element of uncertainty that makes life more interesting and even exciting. Mega hopes, however, are the kind of hopes no one wants. They arise in situations that happen to "other people" until, of course, that situation happens to you.

   Mega hopes go beyond the Mundane and the Moderate, those two levels of hope that we often tie to our status, success, security, and stuff. Mundane and Moderate hopes can catapult or kill our *happiness;* Mega hopes can catapult or kill our life or the life of someone we love. Mundane and Moderate hopes are thus largely *circumstantial* while Mega hopes are largely *existential* and transcendent. Mega hopes can cause an atheist to reach out to God either to curse Him or plead with Him. Let's look at some examples:

- You're flying at 40,000 feet, and one of the plane's engines dies. It's likely you won't live through this, but you hope to God you do.

- You're diagnosed with late-stage cancer. It's likely you won't live through this, but you hope to God you do.

- Your teenager just overdosed on heroin and is in a coma. It's likely he won't come back—or if he comes back, he won't be the same—but you hope to God he makes it.

The stakes are highest with Mega hopes because, in most cases, everything is at stake. Mega hopes force most people to think hard and pray harder. The people who aren't thinking hard and praying harder easily sink into denial. But Mega hopes force most people to reexamine their entire life, their priorities, their purpose, and their beliefs about the **Big Questions.**

Finally, let me ask you this again. Is a Mega hope unique to people of a certain age? No. Does a person's race matter? No. How about that individual's worldview or religion? Nope. It doesn't matter if the person is an agnostic, a Hindu, a Christian, a Muslim, an atheist, or a dude on the couch smoking weed and hoping that the gunshot wound he just got from a rival dealer will not mean his death. Everyone has had or will have Mega hopes.

BEHIND THE CURTAIN

Now, you won't find research articles about these levels of hope. I made them up, but I think they pretty accurately reflect life.

What are we to make of all these observations? These levels of hope may be interesting, but these ideas don't help me *find* or *have* hope. Well, remember what I said about following the *feelings* but ignoring the *beliefs*? Like Danielson (or Daniel san) in *The Karate Kid,* if we want to learn to do crane kicks or catch a fly with chopsticks, we need to first learn how to paint the fence and—as Miyagi taught Daniel—how to wax on and wax off. Likewise, if we want to learn how to recognize fake hope and find real, powerful hope, we need to first learn how to think clearly about these issues. *Understanding* must always precede *application.*

Let's get started by noting three characteristics that the three levels of hope have in common.

1. *UNIVERSAL.* Another observation we've already made is that anyone can have Mundane, Moderate, or Mega hopes, regardless of age, race, gender, or beliefs. This fact is significant because it communicates that having hope is not the exclusive right of only some people or just certain groups. We are all hope-hungry beings. We all need hope to survive. Having hope is a universal desire and need.

2. *WISHING*—and now we're hitting some pay dirt. Synonymous to all the hopes we looked at, from Mundane to Mega, are wishing, wanting, desiring, and positive thinking. We define *wishing* as "feeling or expressing a strong desire or hope for

something that is not easily attainable; wanting something that cannot or probably will not happen." Now there's nothing wrong with wishing and having bright thoughts about the future. Quite the contrary! Staying positive and optimistic can have powerful emotional and physical benefits. The problem comes when mere optimism is all you've got. Positive thinking can only go so far, and many Mega issues require more. Much more. When positive thinking and optimism slide into denial—and that happens often—then a person borders on mild psychosis. Also, positive thinking has little, if any, power especially when it comes to Moderate and Mega hope issues.

3. *MANUFACTURED*. A last feature of all three levels is, they are all self-generated. In other words, they come to mind *and* they stay there. And they are personal and **subjective**:

> "I hope (want/wish) this casserole turns out well."
> "I hope (want/wish) this bank doesn't foreclose on me."
> "I hope (want/wish) this plane lands with only one engine."

I *like* chocolate ice cream. I *wish* there were world peace. I *want* to provide for my family. I *hope* Rebekah gets healed. Again, these are internal, personal, and subjective—and basically, I'm powerless. These hopes/wants/wishes are not able to comfort you as you deal with profound fear, worry, pain, and suffering. Nor do they have any power to change or affect the course of events.

They may affect you (inside) but they won't affect anything else (outside).

I know what you're thinking: *Geez, great. Real hopeful, Joel. What a downer. If I'd had any hope before, you just killed it. I think I'll switch this coffee for a stronger drink.* I know, I know!

But what if there is another level of hope, one that not only transcends all other hopes but is also completely the opposite of subjective, self-manufactured wishful thinking? What if this hope can comfort you however heavy your burden of fear, worry, pain, and suffering is? And what if this hope can actually change the course of future events?

Skeptical? Good. In the rest of this book, I hope to show you how you, too, can do the sweetest crane kick. Keep reading and—as Morpheus told Neo—"I'll show you how deep the rabbit hole goes."

CHAPTER 6

THE HEART'S CRY FOR SOMEONE BIG

A S FAR BACK as we can go in human history, we see global evidence of people crying out to something or someone outside themselves, something much bigger than themselves. Men and women have called upon the sun, the moon, the spirits, the universe, the gods, and *the* God. Children instinctively call out for their parents (who are like God to them), and the parents call up for help to their god—whatever or whoever that may be.

The **Old Testament** says that God *has made everything beautiful in its time. He has also set eternity in the human heart; yet no one can fathom what God has done from beginning to end* (Ecclesiastes 3:11). We all have something built into us, something unique to our human nature not shared by any other creature: God has set eternity in our hearts. What's that mean? I believe it's about a deep awareness that we possess and that equally possesses us.

Whether or not we acknowledge it, we *know* in our heart of hearts there is more to life than what we experience with our five senses. We sense that we are not alone, that there is something—maybe Someone—really, really BIG out there behind the scenes. We *know* that somehow and in some way our physical death is not the end of our story. Complete psychosomatic extinction just *feels* wrong in the same way that thinking there is no God *feels* very wrong (Psalm 14:1). There's something not right about the idea of our extinction, something insidious even. We instinctively sense and intuitively know that we are, somehow, part of a really Big Story that is unfolding. We're not exactly sure of the details, but somehow, we know that we human beings are incredibly special. And—no matter what our professed beliefs—we instinctively call out to the Author of this story for help in times of need.

During the dark chapter of my divorce (leading up to it, during all the proceedings, and afterward), I filled eight spiral-bound notebooks with my reflections on life. Even though I had been a Christian for ten years and even though I had a well-thought-out worldview (I was—to be fancy—epistemically self-aware), I was desperately trying to make sense of life, especially the painful parts. I read books as if my life depended on it... because it kinda did. Desperate times call for desperate measures, as "they" say. Every insight I gained and nugget I discovered, I wrote down and then fleshed out in those journals. Each journal had a different color cover, which became the name for that journal.

In my Black Book journal, I was thinking about this "eternity in the human heart" idea. I wrote:

> There is so much more to life and reality than meets the eye. Every human has felt the pain of this eternity in their hearts. Every human knows, on some level, that they are eternal beings, that there is something special about them, about us. We have this foggy, veiled sense that there is so much more to it all, so much we are missing out on.

Maybe you believe in God, but you're confused or disillusioned. Maybe you don't believe God even exists. Maybe you just don't know. Yet at times you still look up and cry out in your heart for Someone really BIG to help you. Let me give you some examples from my life.

CRYING OUT FOR DAD

As a kid, around seven or eight, I went through a phase I still remember well. My little sister, Jenn, was about five at the time. Before this phase of mine began, Jenn and I shared a bedroom. We had orange bunk beds with baby animal wallpaper. Cute, but not cool. The day came when—at last—I got my own bedroom, between my sister's room and my parents' room.

I remember my first night alone in my new room. My parents were in the living room watching TV, as they did every night. It was so close to my room that if I peeked out my door and down the hall, I could see the whiskers on my dad's big beard.

Well, for some reason, I got scared, and I did what came instinctively—and the following scene played itself out pretty regularly.

"Dad!" I called out, softly—at first. Remember back then when you were absolutely certain a monster of some sort was in your bedroom? Something nefarious was in there with you, just waiting for you to move so it could pounce. You dared not move a muscle, or it would know exactly where you were. You'd get hot and sweaty, but you didn't dare move. (My parents let me watch the original *Poltergeist* when I was a kid. It wrecked me for about ten years.) Was there a killer clown doll under my bed? Was a creature in my closet? Was the bedroom door about to slam shut on its own?

"Daaaaddddd!!".... "DAAADDD!!"

My dad would come in. "What's going on, buddy?"

Now feeling as if I'd been a little overly dramatic, I'd say, "I don't know. I'm just kind of scared."

"What are you scared of?"

"I don't know. I just feel scared."

"There's nothing to be afraid of. Mom and I are right down the hall."

"I know. It's just…"

"Do you want me to sit with you for a bit?"

"Yeah."

My dad would sit in the chair next to my bed for a while, rubbing my back. Dad was there, so I knew that everything in the world would be okay. The evil monsters in my room had fled at his appearance. My room felt safe again.

But then the next night… "Daadd?" "Daaaddd!?" My dad would come in, and we'd go through the same routine. He would sit with me for a while, calm the storm, and go back to the living room.

Next night: "Daadd!?"

This went on for a couple months. I think many times I wasn't even afraid. I just liked having my dad near me. Dad was safe. Dad was powerful. Dad knew everything. Dad saved me.

I never called out for my mom even though she was a great, attentive, and loving mom who fiercely defended me. One day, for instance, I was playing with this kid down the street named Doug. (Every street or neighborhood has a Doug.) Doug was usually mean to me, but I always tried to get in his good graces. Well, on this particular day Doug bit me on the hand. I don't remember why, but he bit me and drew blood. I ran home to show my mom, and she—about a hundred pounds of fury—tore out the front door and stormed down the street. Trailing behind her and holding my bloody hand, I cried, "Mom! Mom! What are you doing? What are you going to do?" I thought she would kill Doug—or at least bite him back.

Mom pounded on Doug's front door. It opened, and there stood Doug's mom. *Dear God,* I thought. Doug's mom towered over my mom. God had built this one like a buffalo! Yet my mom opened a can of verbal whoopas on this hoodlum raiser. I stood there overwhelmed by sheer fear and amazement.

Had that been my dad, he would have sauntered down to Doug's house, rung the doorbell, and calmly talked to Doug's mom about how what Doug had done to me wasn't cool. There probably would have been some apologies and some shaking of hands. That was my dad. My mom, though, was more like the Tasmanian Devil. Screw civility! Her boy was bitten by a bad kid who was being raised by a bad mom. Bad, bad people! So Mom threw a freakin' grenade into their house.

Since I'd seen my mom in action on my behalf, you'd think I'd call out for Mom on those fearful nights. Hey, if a monster had lived in my room, she would have ripped its head off. My dad would have calmly asked it to leave. But I didn't call for Mom. I called for Dad. Every time. Even though my dad was gentle and used treaties instead of grenades, he was still more powerful than Mom. He was still stronger and tougher, and I just knew that monsters feared him more than they feared my mom. Mom could rip heads off; Dad could banish them with a word.[4]

SOCIAL INJUSTICES

Let me give you a few more examples of how we cry out for Someone Powerful to help us.

Spammers and Scammers

I bet you can relate to this one: spam calls and texts to your cell phone. Over the last couple years, at least for Rebekah and me, the number of calls has gotten out of control. I get five to

---

4 Moms may have the final word, however. I think with life-and-death issues, our instinct is to cry out for Mommy. The movie *Saving Private Ryan* powerfully illustrates this reality. I'm thinking of the scene when one of the soldiers (Giovanni Ribisi) sent to find Private Ryan was shot in the stomach. As he lay on the ground, bleeding out, dying, he cried out, "Mamma, Mamma! I want to go home! I want to go home! Mamma, Mamma, Mamma, Mam…." It's a heart-wrenching scene that rings very true to me. You can find it on YouTube by typing in "saving private ryan calling mamma." I also think of my own experience, while going through my divorce and broken in every way, my first instinct was to want my mom.

eight random calls every day. I'm sure you do as well. First Orion, a leading provider of phone call and data transparency solutions, reported that up to 50 percent of U.S. mobile traffic would be scam calls by 2019.[5] That seems about right to me.

If I'm in a pleasant mood when a call comes in, I'll say, "Oh my gosh! There's blood everywhere! I can't believe I did this. There's so much blood! Call Ricky! He'll know what to do!" The spammers always hang up on me. Other times I'll pretend I'm an old Vietnam vet who wants to get a corn dog. I talk like a crotchety old man: "Do you have a corn dog?" Every time they reply, "Uh, excuse me, sir?" "A corn dog! I'm so hungry. I just want a corn dog. You got one?" "Um, I'm sorry, sir. What are you saying? A corn what?" But most of the time when I answer these calls and realize they have duped me, my finger hits the red button, and a little steam escapes from my ears.

I know that there are apps and things to help block this crap. Getting a blocker is on my list of things to do someday. But until then it gets frustrating to receive all these calls. Many times Rebekah and I have cried out, "Someone's got to do something about this! There has to be someone out there who can put a stop to these intrusions!"

A Most Annoying Fact of (SoCal) Life

Another example is traffic. Now, some of you won't be able to relate much to this example, but if you live in Southern California or any other major metropolitan area, traffic makes for a most annoying way of life. Here, destinations that take ten minutes to get to often take 45 minutes, and a 45-minutes-away destination can take two hours. Many times, when Rebekah and I are parked on the freeway, inching along slower than a cockroach, I will—out of exasperation—cry, "Someone's got to do something about this! We can't live this way! There has to be someone out there who can fix this!"

---

5 https://firstorion.com/nearly-50-of-u-s-mobile-traffic-will-be-scam-calls-by-2019/

How Much?!?!

Another example is the cost of living. Here in Southern California, you need at least half a million dollars to get your foot into the real estate market—I'm talking about a starter home! Rebekah and I cry out: "Someone's got to do something about this! The cost of housing, taxes—damn stinking taxes—gas, bills, bills, bills—it's all going up, and my income is going down! We can't live this way indefinitely. There has to be someone out there who can fix this, someone big and powerful who can stem this flow of blood. Help us find some relief, God! Help us!" Ever felt that way?

COSMIC INJUSTICES

The examples we've looked at could be considered social injustices, cultural injustices, even first-world problems. Or things that just plain suck. They range from Mundane to Moderate hope issues.

But what about when you or your child is diagnosed with cancer? What about when your child is born with a severe disability? What about when your spouse leaves you for someone else? What about when someone you love is being destroyed by an addiction, a mental illness, or Alzheimer's? These don't feel like social or cultural injustices. These feel like—these *are*—cosmic injustices. These are Mega.

In these desperate circumstances, we also instinctively cry out, sometimes for help, sometimes in protest, but we don't cry out horizontally. No one on our level is big enough. Rather, we cry out vertically for Someone Big, as in big on a cosmic level. Wanting to understand the loss, the pain, the fear, the suffering, we ask "Why?" We protest and even rage. But from the core of our being—in our heart of hearts—we cry out to God for help. And often that cry issues forth without us uttering a single word.

When I went through the dark chapter of divorce and despair, I found deep comfort in the book of **Psalms**. For the first time, my reading of it wasn't merely academic. These words lived, breathed, and bled. The writers of the Psalms were men like me, fraught with weakness, failure, fear, and pain. They struggled in life, and they struggled with their faith. And they were absolutely honest about all of that. I found great comfort that God put these raw expressions of human frailty in His Word. It's as if God is saying, "It's all right to be you and to come to me all broken, confused, and afraid. I already know that you are a sinner, and I understand what it's like to be human in a fallen world populated by other sinners." Listen to this:

> O LORD, *God of my salvation,*
> *I have cried out day and night before You.*
> *Let my prayer come before You;*
> *Incline Your ear to my cry.*
> *For my soul is full of troubles,*
> *And my life draws near to the grave.*
> *I am counted with those who go down to the pit;*
> *I am like a man who has no strength, adrift among the dead…*
> *My eye wastes away because of affliction.*
> LORD, *I have called daily upon You;*
> *I have stretched out my hands to You….*
> LORD, *why do You cast off my soul?*
> *Why do You hide Your face from me? (Psalm 88:1-5, 9, 14 NKJV)*

Yeah, that's in the Bible. That guy was jacked up, just like me. He felt like God had turned His back on him, just like I've felt. Not only did God allow him to express these feelings, but God seems to be fine with them. Hey, God put it in His Word for us!

HOPING IN GOD KNOWS WHAT

When we talk about *hope*, most people's hope doesn't differ much from my inner cry for someone to fix the problems of cell phone spammers, traffic jams, and the high cost of living. They know what they want, but their hope has no place to take root. Why? Because their hope sits in their head. It starts and stops there. We're made, though, to cry out to Someone Really Big, and that's what I've done because I've put my hope in that Someone Really Big. But many times, when I ask people what they put their hope in, eyes stare, then look away, and shoulders shrug.

We human beings can't live without hope, whether our circumstances are Mundane, Moderate, or Mega. Yet we know that something is missing, something critical. It's like we're in an archery contest, one that our lives depend on, but there are no targets. Zero. Huh? But we need to fire our arrows. We're *made* to do so. We have a quiver of arrows on our backs and a bow in our hands. We're in a situation that requires us to shoot. But there aren't any targets! So we stand there, not understanding what or where to shoot our arrows. We thus feel a deep sense of existential angst that characterizes our entire culture, maybe world.

Yet because we are hope-hungry beings who cannot live without hope, we shoot. We have to. A tree. A rock. A bird. A person. A movement. A cause. A philosophy. A religion. Arrows fly around like confetti as we shoot.

I believe, however, that *another kind* of hope exists. A straightforward, easy-to-access hope. Before I get to that, though, I want to explore some of the more common hopes we fire at, many of which people rarely even recognize as the source of their hope. Some of these may even surprise you.

PART TWO

WHEN OUR HOPES DISAPPOINT

CHAPTER 7

HOPES THAT DISAPPOINT PART 1

KNOW SOMETHING ABOUT you that you may not know about yourself. I know something about you that, actually, you may vigorously contest. I know that you are a deeply religious person. I don't know you personally, but I can make that statement about anyone because... Yep, *all people are religious beings.* That's another way of saying that we are hope-hungry beings.

Okay, okay, let's slow this train down a bit. I know. I just threw a huge claim out there, and some of you jumped back with your dukes up. Let me explain what I mean by *religious.*

In this context, I'm not using the word *religious* the way most people think of it. I'm using it more philosophically and therefore more accurately. You see, I'm not saying that I know that you go to church on Sundays. I'm not saying that you read the Bible or believe in the **Trinity**. I'm not even saying that you follow any prescribed set of moral rules, life principles, or clearly defined **doctrines.**

What I am saying is that everyone has a worldview. And—as I've said—at the center of your worldview are your core beliefs about ultimate reality, knowledge, ethics, and purpose. Those core beliefs inform your ultimate commitment and enable you to make some sense of, well, everything.

At the very least, every worldview must answer these four ultimate questions:

QUESTION 1: *WHERE AM I?* Are you in the Matrix? Are you someone's dream and everything you think you know is only ten seconds long? Are you in God's created reality that He sustains by His power? Are you existing in what is nothing more than a cosmic accident, resulting from a Big Bang, and everything is just matter-in-motion? Is everything we experience mere illusion and we can't experience the ultimate reality? *Where are you?*

QUESTION 2: *WHO AM I?* Are you a god? Are you just a biological bag of stuff, a chemical cocktail responding to various stimuli? Are you an independent (autonomous), totally free being? Are you a special creation made in God's image? Are you nothing more than a spark of a much greater fire? Are you a reincarnation from something else? *Who are you?*

QUESTION 3: *WHAT'S THE PROBLEM?* Or is there no problem? Are problems and suffering mere illusion? Is our selfishness the problem? Do our problems stem from ignorance, a lack of education in what matters? Do our problems arise because we rebel against God? Do we suffer because God is vindictive and sadistic or maybe just indifferent? Do we struggle and suffer because of capitalism or socialism or poverty or inequality or...? *What's the problem?*

QUESTION 4: *WHAT'S THE SOLUTION?* Is the solution more knowledge, more education? Do we need to sharpen our ability to reason? Do we need more love and acceptance? Will our suffering end if we turn to God and follow Him? Maybe the solution is to believe there is no problem? Would more money—or maybe economic equality—solve the problems? Or is the solution to get rid of all collective belief in God or religion? *What's the solution?*

Believe it or not, you have answers to these big questions whether you've ever articulated them or not. Your answers stem from your worldview, and your worldview is your *ultimate faith commitment* that you hold to with religious tenacity. *That* thing or *that* idea or *that* philosophy is the god you're holding on to by faith. This faith commitment guides what you give your time, money, and attention to. It's what you use to interpret your experiences and make sense of life. You fall back on this worldview when life falls apart. And all those actions are acts of worship: you are bowing down, submitting to, and deferring to what is most important to you. Whatever you worship—whatever you give ultimate allegiance to—*that* is your god. Do you now see how each of us really is a deeply religious being?

Even still, some of you may recoil at this line of reasoning. Maybe thinking of yourself as a religious person who worships anything is outrageous, degrading, blasphemous, or insulting to you. But if that's your reaction, I simply see you as more devout than the average person who couldn't care less either way. Violent inner reactions reveal much about the degree of our ultimate commitments.

LEAVING BEHIND MUNDANE AND MODERATE HOPES

Whether or not we realize it, our hope is rooted in our deepest faith commitments. We rarely see this reality evidenced in our Mundane hope issues, but we start to see it in our Moderate hopes, and we almost always recognize it in our Mega hopes. Our Mega hope issues are the acid test of the effectiveness and power of what we place our hope in.

Not that Mundane or Moderate hope issues are unimportant,

but I think most people will agree that those issues rarely, if ever, have nearly the intensity of Mega hope needs. So for the rest of this book, we will leave the Mundane and Moderate hopes behind. After all, whenever we talk about needing effective hope—*real* hope—we are usually referring to Mega hope issues anyway.

THE BIG FIVE

But what exactly underlies or is at the heart of our Mega hopes? I see at least five desires for knowledge (see Appendix 1). Ultimately, we want to know the following:

- **WE ARE NOT ALONE.** We want to know that there is Someone Big out there who listens, who cares, and who can actually do something—even something miraculous—to help.

- **LIFE HAS MEANING.** We want to know that life is not pointless; that we really matter; and that life has an ultimate meaning that gives us purpose on this earth.

- **SUFFERING HAS A PURPOSE.** We want to know that loss, sorrow, hardship, trials, and pain are not pointless, that something good can come out of our dark times even if the circumstances don't resolve the way we want them to.

- **WE CAN FIND THE POWER.** We want to know that we can find inner comfort, strength, and peace that will get us through Mega storms.

- **THERE IS LIFE AFTER DEATH:** We want to know that, when we die physically, somehow we don't cease to exist; somehow we will live on after death; and somehow wherever we are living will be a better place.

One or more of these Big Five is at the heart of all Mega hope issues. I encourage you to read through the list one more time. They will appear again and again throughout the rest of this book.

THE GODS OF OUR CULTURE

What we hope in is what we trust. Let me expand that thought so it doesn't sound so much like a riddle: Whatever we consider the source of our hope is what we are choosing to trust. Whenever our lives are in jeopardy, we look to this source of hope—in which we trust—for help, for rescue, and, yes, for salvation. Whatever these sources are will then act as our gods. But not all gods are equal, nor are all worthy of our trust. Some things we trust actually turn out to be demons, figuratively speaking.

So, what are these gods I'm speaking of? In the order of importance and prevalence, here is my list of what I consider the predominant gods in our culture today:

1. Technology

2. Money

3. Government

4. Science

5. Education

6. Spiritualism

7. Philosophy

8. Religion

Space prevents any kind of in-depth examination or critique of each of these gods. So below I offer only a brief overview of these sources of faith, trust, and hope that our culture relies on.

TECHNOLOGY

Science tempted me for first place on this list, but I don't think science is as sexy as it was in times past when people believed that science would solve all our problems. To be sure, science is on the list here, and I'll address that, but technology is the application of scientific findings. Technology, as we all know, is developing at a blistering pace. Its results are so impressive and so effective that it's hard not to crown technology king.

While the actual practice or thought of science impacts few of us, technology has a thousand tentacles tightly wrapped around every aspect of our life and every second of our day. From the printing press to cell phones, lightbulbs to MRI machines, technology shapes how we perceive reality. It changes not only *what* things we think about but also *how* we think.

In what I consider his most insightful book, *Technopoly: The Surrender of Culture to Technology,* the late Neil Postman wrote this:

> Technopoly is a state of culture. It is also a state of mind. It consists in the deification of technology, which means that the culture seeks its authorization in technology, finds its satisfactions in technology, and takes it orders from technology. This requires the development of a new kind of social order, and of necessity leads to the rapid dissolution of much that is associated with traditional beliefs. Those who feel most comfortable in Technopoly are those who are convinced that technical progress is humanity's supreme achievement and the instrument by which our most profound dilemmas may be solved.[6]

Our culture has deified technology, believing that it can accomplish any feat and enable us to overcome any problem. As

6 Neil Postman, *Technopoly* (NY: Vintage Books, 1993), 71.

Postman said, we seek its authorization, we look to it for satisfaction, and we even take our orders from technology.

Medical technology is one area of advancement so impressive it's hard not to regard it as a source of hope. Rebekah and I know this well: medical technology has beaten back most of her cancer and saved her life. In fact, I'm writing this from the City of Hope cancer hospital, where in a couple hours Rebekah will have ten million genetically modified T-cells injected into her brain. The DNA of these T-cells was extracted from her body, modified in a laboratory with the non-threatening part of the HIV virus, and then mutated into cancer-finding and cancer-fighting warrior cells. It's science fiction stuff.

I think it's safe to say that much of our modern culture—maybe most of it—finds purpose, guidance, satisfaction, beliefs, and hope in the many forms of technology, both the seen and the unseen. But can technology, with all its impressive advancements and abilities, provide us with real hope, with a hope strong enough to meet us in the middle of the Mega and especially at the crossroads we encounter there? The answer is no.

Technology is wonderful, but it's just an enormous box of tools. Technology provides no philosophy for life, no **grand narrative** that offers wisdom, and no worldview that provides purpose. Technology cannot provide moral guidance, nor can it tell us what we ought to do and ought not do. Technology cannot comfort you in the middle of the night, deep in your soul, when the world is crashing down on you or when the engine of your plane decides to quit. Technologies come and go: they are born and they die just like we do. And if there is an afterlife, technology can't get you there.

In addition to those major shortcomings, the expansion of technology brings a host of additional problems and anxieties.

New technologies bring higher bills and require more of our money. Technologies can breed new and unnecessary longings, desires, and wants in us, often exacerbating the anxiety and stress we already feel. Millions of people are addicted to social media yet, like cigarettes, it's the very thing that's harming them the most. After all, social media has been aptly described as "a turbo-charged, precision instrument for social comparison unlike anything in human history."[7]

Along with all the blessings of technology come feelings of inferiority, envy, anxiety, and depression. In short, you can feel like a real loser. Our culture has even coined an acronym for this: FOMO—Fear Of Missing Out. Aware of this potential impact on us, we nevertheless bury our faces in the screens and keep going back for more.

Okay, technology can provide types of hope, like letting us look into the human body to discover problems or in connecting us socially, but these types are small, circumstantial, and time-bound. Scan back a few pages to The Big Five, those human desires for knowledge that are at the heart of all Mega hope. Technology does not speak to any of The Big Five fundamental issues of life.[8]

MONEY

Money—economic security—is clearly a powerful god in our modern culture. It's one of the easiest to understand, and most everywhere we look we see it being worshiped. We all kinda know this, so I won't belabor the point. Money allows a person to gain all the technology desired—and so much more. Heck, if you have enough money, you can buy yourself a new kidney or even a new kid. No doubt you can buy yourself a new lover. In

---

7 https://www.psychologytoday.com/us/articles/201711/the-comparison-trap
8 Far more could be said on this issue, but space forbids. I will simply recommend Neal Postman's book *Technopoly*.

our culture money equates to power, status, position, and security. Money is indeed a powerful god.

And money is not a new god. Written thousands of years ago, the Old Testament book of Proverbs says, *Will you set your eyes on that which is not? For riches certainly make themselves wings; they fly away like an eagle toward heaven* (23:5). Still, people place hope in riches.

And you don't have to have money to seek hope in money. Perhaps for most human beings throughout history, money has meant food, shelter, and basic survival. Money, however, has a powerful allure. After all, poor people don't spend millions of dollars every month buying lottery tickets for food, shelter, and basic survival. They're looking for something else. They're looking for the hope of final fulfillment and what they see as salvation. But it's a fools errand and a hope that will disappoint.

Don't believe me? We only need to listen to the scores of people who have gained substantial wealth and fame in hopes that it would fulfill them and save them. Their stories are all very similar. They had all the luxuries of life yet felt emptier, more isolated, and more depressed than ever. Celebrity suicides confirm this. Money is a splendid thing that can help us and enhance our life in many wonderful ways, but like technology, money is to be just a tool for life. Money cannot provide sufficient hope for any of The Big Five Mega hope issues.

GOVERNMENT

For the too many people unable to acquire wealth for even the basics, government and all its social welfare programs can be a god. From birth to death, millions of people look to the government to take care of them. But that's not the whole story. Too many of these people feel *entitled* to such care as if it's a basic human right. I don't get this—and I don't find any rationale for it in any worldview, be it **atheism** or any form of **theism**. Yet many people feel and think that they are entitled to have basically whatever they want provided by the government. Ironically, big government itself has fostered this kind of thinking.

Again, go back and review The Big Five. Can the government—any government—deal with any of those Mega hope needs and issues? No. Human government can help with some basic needs for survival, but it can't tend to the more important issues of life. Government is a disinterested parent that gives out allowances but cares not a whit about you.

SCIENCE

Now we come to science, to Science the Almighty. Science is the default for many people: "I don't believe in God; I believe in science." I think of the scene from that brilliant movie *Nacho Libre* where Nacho's wrestling buddy, Esqueleto, tells Nacho why he never got baptized: "I only believe in science."

I believe that people who default to science as their god haven't really thought through the matter. You see, most people I've talked to—or whom I've heard talking—about science actually know little about what science is. A lot of what gets called science today is not science at all. Working with numbers or mathematics is not science, or else accountants would be scientists. Technological tools are also not science. To be sure, the process and discoveries of scientific investigation are most impressive and impactful. I'm not at all disparaging or downplaying the awesome work of science. My wife is alive today because of discoveries made by hundreds of scientists. I would venture to say that half of America is alive because of some scientific discovery made at some point in the history of science! Yet like technology and money, science—with its power and all its significant discoveries—is, basically, another tool for life.

What, then, is science? At its most basic level, science is a very human endeavor to discover reliable and repeatable patterns of causation in the natural world. That's it. Science is basically us trying to figure out how this big ol' crazy world works. When we discover a reliable and repeatable pattern of inference or causation, we call that a "law" like the law of gravity. Once we discern these laws, we use what we now know and corral the power of what we have discovered in thousands of ways, from treating infections to landing on the moon. Science truly is awesome, but it is severely limited in its ability to provide the hope that we humans need as we face the important issues of life. Science, for instance, will not keep you from committing suicide, nor will it lift you out of the blackness of depression when a loved one dies.

Like technology—every form of which is an application of science—science provides no philosophy for life, no grand narrative that offers wisdom, and no worldview that provides purpose.[9] Science cannot provide moral guidance, nor can it tell us what we ought or ought not to do. Science cannot comfort you in the middle of the night, deep in your soul, when the world is crashing down on you or when the engine of your plane suddenly stops working. Sciences come and go: they are born and they die just like we do. And if there is an afterlife, science remains silent. Science is wonderful and amazing, but it is an insufficient source of hope.

These four so far—technology, money, government, and science—are powerful gods to many people today. But when it comes

9 This sentence may seem confusing or wrong to many people. Remember, science is a tool. Individual scientists pursuing scientific endeavors will have their own worldview that may provide them wisdom and direction for life. But scientists don't get these ideas and beliefs from science; quite the contrary, the scientists already have these beliefs and bring them into their practice of science. But, as history clearly shows, scientific discovery works whether a person is a theist, an atheist, or an agnostic. Yet science itself is not a worldview; rather, our worldviews influence our interpretation of scientific tests and results.

to providing hope strong enough to help us through all of life's issues (including The Big Five), each one of these gods falls way short. In their own ways, each one promises hope it cannot fulfill.

But we humans don't like giving up. We are ingenious in our attempts to find hope. We just have to shoot those arrows. We can't help it. So maybe these four gods can't do it—but maybe something else can. Maybe we can find real hope in education or in spiritualism, in philosophy or maybe in religion. In the next chapter we'll explore each of these gods, and maybe we'll find sufficient ground for real hope.

CHAPTER 8

HOPES THAT DISAPPOINT PART 2

L ET'S JUMP RIGHT in and explore four more cultural gods. Maybe one of them will give us real hope.

EDUCATION

We could also use the label *knowledge*, *reason*, or *progress*. This idea and belief that more knowledge can solve all our problems has its roots in the **Enlightenment** movement that started in Europe around 1650 and wound down around 1800. This way of thinking, with its emphasis on reason and science, began with the philosophers. It then spread to all other parts of academia and eventually into popular culture.[10]

The big idea behind this period is that humans can discover truths about reality, knowledge, and ethics apart from any kind of alleged **divine revelation**. Some thinkers looked to the natural world to prove God's existence, but other thinkers did away with belief in God altogether. Whether or not God exists was not the dominant idea. The dominant idea was that man in his

---

10 To see how this philosophy has played out from ancient Rome up to our present day, read Francis Schaeffer's classic *How Shall We Then Live*.

own power can discover truth, morals, and meaning. People also believed that man (women had little influence during this time) would figure out how to solve our greatest problems, answer life's greatest questions, and thus usher in a utopian era of peace, prosperity, and happiness. *Hey! We got this!*

Enlightenment ideas and attitudes came to America with many of our founders and were reinforced later by American thinkers and philosophers. One main idea behind this Enlightenment **humanism**—a philosophy that, as the word suggests, elevates humans above any divine force or being—is that all people are basically good at heart. The reason we make bad decisions, hurt other people, get addicted...whatever... is because we lack certain knowledge, and had we known it, we would have chosen otherwise. This idea goes all the way back to the Greek philosopher Plato, one of the foremost philosophers rediscovered in the Renaissance and the Enlightenment periods.

The unimaginable horrors of World Wars I and II, however, put a big dent in this theory: we saw all too clearly that modern educated people can act like monsters. Yet this idea or, rather, this **presupposition** that we are all good at heart and that we have the power within ourselves to solve all problems and create an earthly utopia is still strong today. It's ingrained in our theories of education, our public school systems, and our institutions of higher education. The thinking still is "The more we know, the more ethical and more altruistic we will be. We can do it!" We can place hope in our abilities to learn, grow, and solve problems. Well, that's the idea anyway....

I know from my personal experience that education isn't the answer to all our problems. I know a lot of stuff. I've studied religion, philosophy, history, sociology, psychology, and ethics for twenty years now. Has it made me a better person? For sure.

But I also know my own heart. There's still darkness in there despite all my schooling. While I believe I have many good and noble qualities, I also know that in my heart, there's **evil**. Want some evidence? I know what's right, and I don't always do it. Sometimes I deliberately choose to do what I know is absolutely wrong. At times I'm selfish, devious, deceitful, gross, and mean. It's not like I'm ignorant that such things aren't good. I *know*—and I'm like that anyway! And guess what? You're no different.

Jesus taught something that may make us cringe, but in our heart of hearts, we know His words are true. Where does evil come from? He says, *"Out of the heart proceed evil thoughts, murders, adulteries, fornications, thefts, false witness, blasphemies"* (Matthew 15:19).

I'm guilty of all those things by either outward action or inward thought. Everyone is guilty—and those who deny the evil in their heart are lying to themselves. "The evil and darkness of this world comes to a great degree from within us," says Timothy Keller. He continues:

> **Martin Luther** [the 15th-century reformer] taught that human nature is *in curvatus in se,* curved in on itself. We are so instinctively and profoundly self-centered that we don't believe we are. And this curved-in-ness is a source of a vast amount of the suffering and evil we experience, from the violence and genocides in the headlines down to the reason your marriage is so painful.[11]

Education and learning are important and good, but let us not fool ourselves into thinking we can solve or prevent all evils by acquiring facts. Our problems are profoundly deeper and more severe than we realize. Education can help us become better

---

11 Timothy Keller, *Walking with God Through Pain and Suffering* (NY: Penguin Books, 2015), 123.

citizens, and in this sense, education is yet another tool for life. But human reason and knowledge are not a sufficient source of Mega hope. Learning more facts about the world doesn't help us with The Big Five.

Maybe we need to look within and get in touch with our spiritual side. Or maybe we need to look outward into the universe for help and hope.

SPIRITUALISM

Being "spiritual" is quite popular right now. In some respects, it's even becoming cool in mainstream culture. Many people realize that technology, money, education, government, and science can't provide meaning, fulfillment, or hope. They realize that we are more than machines, more than mere matter-in-motion. They realize that there is something very special about us and about this world we find ourselves in.

While I've talked to many people who say, "I don't believe in God; I believe in science," I've talked to even more who say, "I'm not religious; I'm spiritual." What does that mean? Well, let me share a little secret here: it means nothing. It's called "pabulum." But, okay, what are these people *trying* to say? They are trying to disassociate themselves from what we consider "traditional religion," a phrase that simply means Christianity. These people say, "I don't believe in the Bible, I don't go to church on Sundays, I don't pray to Jesus or some old man in the sky. I don't believe in any of those things, but I am very spiritual nonetheless. Nature is my church, I am or some guru is my bible, and meditation, contemplation, and **mindfulness** is my prayer."

What, then, do "spiritual" people believe? Well, that's the thing. They can believe anything, really. They can believe that we are all sparks of energy trying to find our way back to the

Ultimate One; they can believe that the Universe is a living Mind[12] that we can interact with; they can believe that there is a Higher Power of sorts out there; they can believe that aliens planted us here billions of years ago and still monitor us; they can believe that we are all minor gods; they can believe any of a hundred other ideas. Really, what they believe doesn't matter. The appeal of being "spiritual" is that you get to make up and believe whatever you want. As a result, you can still live however you want to live. You don't have the stigma of being "religious," yet you are acknowledging that we humans are spiritual beings. It's an attempt of being committed to something spiritual that doesn't require anything from you.

So how is the Bible different? Well, one of its unique and revolutionary features is its claim to be a ***propositional revelation***. What does that phrase even mean? Let's look at the two words in reverse.

FIRST, THE BIBLE CLAIMS TO BE A SPECIAL *REVELATION* FROM GOD HIMSELF. It says that, yes, God exists, and He is not silent. He is not some nebulous "Higher Power" out there; He's also not the Man Upstairs, an impersonal force, or some vague Universal Intelligence. What else could God be, then? God is a person.

This idea of special revelation means that God has not left us to our own devices; He has not abandoned us as cosmic orphans. *Special revelation* means that God has spoken to us, and He has done so through various means. The primary way God has spoken to us is through His prophets and apostles, and they spoke as God's guiding Spirit instructed. These men wrote what they called "the Word of God" or what we call today the Bible

---

12 Adherents of this type of thought will usually capitalize words like *Universal Intelligence*. The late philosopher and theologian Francis Schaeffer pointed out years ago that this is a semantic trick to ascribe a sort of divinity to a made-up word or concept. The capital letters also help the adherents feel spiritual and reverent.

(the word itself means "book"). The Bible calls this writing process *divine inspiration.*

SECOND, THIS DIVINE REVELATION IS *PROPOSITIONAL*. What does that mean? Well, a propositional statement is true or false; it can't be both. This either/or dichotomy is built on the law of non-contradiction. *Elvis is alive and well in Arizona in 2019* is a proposition that is either true or false. This idea—not the Elvis idea! the propositional idea—is more important than you may first realize. Why? Because propositions give us knowledge. True propositional statements give us truth, and this truth tells us about the nature of ultimate reality, about what we can know, and about how we ought to live. Basically, propositional statements define good and evil.

Now back to the popular ideas of God being a Higher Power, a force, the One, or the Universal Intelligence. What are we supposed to do with that? There is no revelation, so the only option is guessing and endless speculation. We can make up whatever we think God is or—more to the point—what we want God to be. Rather than coming to God on His terms and allowing God to tell us who He is, we can make up what this Higher Power is—and is all about—according to our own desires and lifestyle.

Without propositional revelation, we have no basis for ethical standards. Who's to say what's right and what's wrong? To have moral absolutes, we need an established universal and absolute standard that we all recognize and can appeal to. Without that, we'd potentially be dealing with some six billion conflicting opinions... and utter chaos.

But we have the Bible, written by men who were led by God's Spirit. Wouldn't you rather listen to God and let Him tell you who He is, what He's like, and what He desires from us? Wouldn't you rather let God the Creator tell you what ultimate reality is, what the meaning of life is, and how you should live your life? Seems like a better choice to me.

In contrast, a generic belief in a Higher Power, a Cosmic Force, the Man Upstairs, or Universal Intelligence is not sufficient for knowledge, truth, meaning, morals, or hope. There's no substance to that spirituality because there's only silence. There's no knowledge of truth because there's no propositional revelation. There's no moral standard because Universal Intelligence is amoral. When you find yourself in the hospital facing death, Universal Mind or Intelligence will bring you zero comfort, courage, or hope.

PHILOSOPHY

Maybe we can find real hope in philosophy. I'll cut to the chase here: we can't. I've studied philosophy for the last fifteen years. I did my undergraduate degree in philosophy at a **secular** university. I love studying and learning about the history of philosophy and about particular philosophers. I remember being several years into my major, and I felt like my life was drying up. Philosophy had nothing to offer me. It's a dusty graveyard, a barren wasteland.

And no wonder. You see, one task of the philosopher is to find the problems and inconsistencies in other philosophies. So an individual thinker comes along and posits a theory of reality or **ethics** or mind, and the next group of thinkers annihilates it. That's the history of philosophy. It is a path of dismantling and destroying.

Anyway, I took several courses on the history of philosophy, but I remember one in particular. It was a very broad course. We started with the early **Greek philosophers** (meaning before Socrates), and as the semester unfolded, we worked our way up to the present, leaving in our wake a cemetery overcrowded by dead and discarded theories.

On one of the last days of class, I raised my hand: "We've worked through the entire history of philosophy and destroyed every philosophy we've seen. What's left now?"

The professor smiled and stared at me. "I don't know," he said.

So, I ask, is philosophy even important? Absolutely! Do we need it? Again, absolutely. Is it helpful? Very much so. But can it give us any kind of hope? Absolutely not.

Geez, what's left then? Only religion. Could religion hold the solution? Maybe religious people really do have hope.

RELIGION

First, know that I make a distinction between those people who hold to a religious philosophy and practice certain prescribed religious ordinances and other people who claim to *know* God and have a living relationship with God. This section will focus on the former.

Within that category of people, I see two types of religious folk. I consider the first type a *cultural* believer: a person can be a cultural Christian, a cultural Catholic, a cultural Muslim, or a cultural Jew. If you were to ask these people if they believe in God or hold to any religious persuasion, they would say, "Yes, I'm Muslim" or "Yes, I'm a Methodist" or "Yes, I'm Catholic" or "Yes, I'm Buddhist." That's pretty much all they could say. You see, these cultural believers grow up within a particular religion and its corresponding practices (going to Mass, the Temple, etc.), but they are nominal believers in and practitioners of that religion. Nothing in their lifestyle suggests they are genuine followers. This religious connection is just part of their culture whether their culture of origin (their family) or their surrounding culture (a Muslim neighborhood, for example).

In contrast to these cultural believers but still not knowing God are those religious folks who take their religion seriously. They practice the prescribed ordinances and rituals of their faith. They try hard to lead upright lives, and they may even pride themselves on their success. These people often do many good works like feeding the homeless or helping at shelters, hospitals, and retirement homes. They may give money to their organization and other good causes. They try hard to abstain from certain "worldly" activities like R-rated movies, secular music, fashion magazines, vulgar language, and any sexual activity outside of marriage. They may pray, but their prayers are often either memorized, read from a book, or part of a certain ritual (saying the Rosary, for example). Their houses will often be adorned with religious icons, relics, plaques, statues, and art. They may fight for the unborn and promote family values.

By all outward appearances, these individuals seem very religious, sincere, and devout. We would consider them "good people," and by human standards, they are. Their religion is a very important part of their life, it shapes their identity, and it may even be the source of their primary identity.

Alright, Joel, so what's the problem here? Well, for many people, religion meets the needs of some of The Big Five. Like we can know—or at least choose to believe—that we are not alone in this overwhelming cosmos and that life has an ultimate meaning. This is one reason religion is so powerful: it seems to meet many of our deepest needs, and it provides a degree of hope for our Mega hope issues.

My problem, however—or, maybe I should say, my concern— is threefold. My first and primary concern is whether these religious, sincere, devout, and good people really *know* God. **Buddhism**, for example, doesn't have a god and is thus more aligned with atheism. Buddhism is more about moral philosophy than it is about **ontological** theology. Religious, sincere, devout, and good people who are Buddhist will not come to know God.

This issue about really knowing God is also where Islam parts ways with Christianity and Judaism. Islam teaches that God— **Allah**—is not personally knowable. According to **Isma'lilism**, God is absolutely transcendent and unknowable.[13] Allah is *wholly other*. Thus, Islam is more about brute submission and white-knuckle obedience than it is about **redemption** or any kind of personal loving relationship with God. In Judaism and Christianity, God (or **Yahweh**) is personal and relational. He is also transcendent (outside all creation) at the same time that He is equally **immanent** and therefore knowable. The God of Judeo-Christianity is intimately involved in every aspect of His creation, including our daily lives and little concerns. The God of the Bible *wants* us to know Him and walk with Him, an idea that would make little sense to a religious, sincere, devout Muslim.

My second concern has to do with the third and fourth world-view questions we looked at earlier: *What's the problem?* and *What's the solution?*

Eastern religions often deny that a problem even exists. All is an illusion, including our pain and suffering. Deeming everything an illusion is a denial of reality and a denial of our own human experience. So, with its call to people to abandon all hope and give in to whatever is, Buddhism neither embraces reality as being real or encourages followers to act like responsible adults.

Christianity parts with Islam, Judaism, and even Catholicism

---

13 Farhad Daftary, *Ismaili History and Intellectual Traditions* (UK: Routledge, 2017.).

when we ask *What's the problem?* and *What's the solution?* [14] Christianity, based on biblical revelation, has its own distinct answers to these questions.

One of the key distinctions between Christianity and all other world religions is how a person can become right with God, gain good standing with the Almighty, and be accepted by Him. The problem is a problem with us. We are guilty of sin. And of unbelief. Or of just ignoring our Creator God. Instead, we see ourselves as god and do what seems right in our own eyes.

Except for Christianity, all of the world's major religions and belief systems teach that we human beings can attain a right relationship with God—we can appease God—by our efforts and good works. (Christianity focuses on what God did for us. More on this to come.)

The focus on our working and earning a place in **heaven** anticipates a moment of judgment: Will God say, "You're in! You did enough. Just barely, but I'm rounding up"? All major theistic religions believe in such a final judgment, that God will judge us and weigh our good deeds against our bad deeds. Picture America's scales of justice. When it comes to that final judgment, we hope that our goodness outweighs our badness because the eternal consequences are severe if it doesn't.

Now, many people aren't concerned about that judgment because they assume they are good. Oh, they've made some stupid mistakes now and then, but compared to other people, these folks are doing great. Yet because it's easy to find other people who are "badder" than we are, this horizontal view gives us false confidence. But if we realize that God is **perfect** and **holy**, that He Himself is the standard for goodness, and we measure actions

---

14 Catholicism is Christian in that Catholic theology holds to the key fundamentals of the Christian faith. I don't want to give the impression that I think Catholicism is a completely different religion. But I believe that Catholic theology diverges significantly from historic biblical orthodoxy when it comes to the issue of how a person comes to salvation and is ultimately able to enter heaven.

and our thoughts next to Him, that vertical view changes everything. Our situation gets scary at that point.

How are we going to be forgiven for all the nasty stuff we've done—and will do?[15] The world's religions offer nothing more than the cross-your-fingers hope that our good outweighs our bad. But that kind of comparison doesn't even work here on earth. Why would it work with a holy God? Think about it. You get charged with theft and a brutal assault. The jury finds you guilty, and you now stand before the judge for sentencing. She asks if you have anything to say before she delivers her verdict.

"Uh, yes, Your Honor. I want to add that for 15 years I've volunteered at the local food bank, I've volunteered at my local YMCA for the past two years, and I recently rescued two stray dogs. I've basically been a good person. So I ask you to consider all that and set me free."

"Well, that's commendable," the judge says, "but that does not excuse the bad you have done, or wash away your guilt, or undo the crimes you're convicted of and the consequences of those crimes. Look over at your victims. You have financially ruined several families and physically impaired one woman. Where is their justice? If I were to let you go because you've done some good things in the past, who will—as payment—suffer the consequences of the heinous crimes you've already committed? If I were to let you go, I would be doing a huge injustice. In fact, I myself would be guilty of abusing your victims all over again."

This "hope" is what the major world religions offer. They bank on God, the Judge, overlooking their mistakes and sweeping them under the cosmic rug. But if God is a good Judge, He must respond to all violations of His law: He must enforce **justice** by

---

15 This gets even scarier when we learn that God not only evaluates us on what we *do* but also by the way we *think*.

following through on the consequences of failing to live according to the standards of justice He established.

Back to The Big Five. Yes, the major religions of the world can offer insight into some of them... sort of... but not all simultaneously and without anomalies. Trusting in yourself to earn God's acceptance and eternal life is a most frightening strategy. I'll tell you now, I would never make it! I'm a goner if that is my only hope. I know myself, I know my heart, and I know what I've done and thought, things no one but God knows about. Relying on myself to be good enough to make it into heaven is a bet I don't want to wager on. There's no hope in that scenario. Only dread.

But suppose that some kind of heaven or life after death exists. Who populates it? I see now a dilemma. A dilemma for God.

In fact, maybe God has a bigger problem to figure out than we do: *How can God remain just and yet pardon or justify all our wrongdoing and evil? How can God ensure that justice is satisfied and evil is punished without punishing the guilty?* We'll come back to this issue down the road. But right now, notice the tension.

And that tension is a factor in my conclusion that religion can be helpful, but like the rest of the gods we've surveyed, religion doesn't provide a real, lasting, absolute hope that we can bank on now. Further, like technology, religion can prompt serious issues of anxiety, fear, shame, insecurity, and even harmful attempts to rid and cleanse oneself of sin.

As we near the end of this discussion, I freely admit that these summaries are oversimplifications. My goal was to provide a general survey of our culture's main gods. Each has been evaluated—*Does this god offer hope, real hope, for Mega issues?*—and found wanting. Each turns out to be a god that promises hope but doesn't come through. Instead, each reflects a human attempt to rely on ourselves to find a universal, an ideal, a stan-dard, and a worldview that will provide meaning, morals, truth, and hope. And none does so. The graphic below shows these gods we turn to with Mundane, Moderate, and Mega hopes. We have to cast our hopes onto *something*—we can't help it—but all these *somethings* are **finite**. By that I mean these so-called gods are limited, bound by the constraints and built-in decay of our **time/space continuum**.

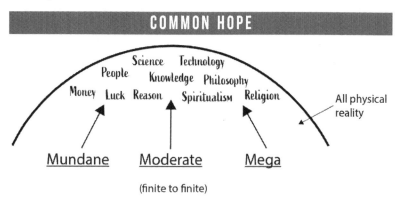

COMMON HOPE

Science Technology
People Knowledge Philosophy
Money Luck Reason Spiritualism Religion

All physical reality

Mundane   Moderate   Mega

(finite to finite)

So I ask again: What if there is another kind of hope? What if there is a hope that doesn't begin with us, doesn't start in our own minds, doesn't rely on our ingenuity or power or connec-tions or education or efforts? What if there is another kind of hope that isn't simply positive thinking, optimism, or wishing? Or what if there is a hope that can absolutely handle Mundane, Moderate, and Mega hope issues? What if there's a hope that also satisfies The Big Five?

That's the Hope we turn to now.

CHAPTER 9

ANOTHER KIND OF HOPE

Y ALL-TIME FAVORITE movie is actually three: *The Lord of the Rings* trilogy based on the novels of J. R. R. Tolkien. These movies have it all: drama, action, adventure, humor, romance, and horror. You get all genres packed into one story. But for me, the most compelling aspect of these movies is the Grand Epic, the Cosmic Story, behind the basic plot. Something really, really BIG is going on behind the scenes.

A couple weeks ago, Rebekah and I had a *Lord of the Rings* party: we spent the weekend watching all three movies in a row. I hadn't seen them in a few years, so I paid close attention to the dialogue.

The week had been very difficult, very painful, especially for Rebekah. We had learned that the clinical trial she had been part of for the preceding five weeks wasn't working. This trial was the CAR-T Cell Therapy I mentioned earlier. At the start of the process, a surgeon implanted a catheter tube into Rebekah's brain. Doctors and researchers then harvested millions of her white blood cells, genetically modified them in a lab, and infused them back into her brain. These modified cells were engineered to be cancer-fighting warrior cells that could attack the tumors in her brain. It's revolutionary medicine, and Rebekah was about the fourth person in all the United States to try it for breast cancer that had spread to the brain. This clinical trial could potentially eradicate all her cancer. Everyone—the doctors, nurses, and researchers—were all excited and hopeful, and everyone expected this treatment to do it for Rebekah.

Our hopes were up too. Both of us were excited. She did five infusions over five weeks. With each infusion, ten million T-Cells were injected directly into her brain. Each infusion had some brutal side effects, but we pushed forward in hope.

But after a brain MRI, we learned not only that the treatment wasn't working, but also that new tumors had emerged as the old ones grew. The clinical trial stopped. It was over. We were done. Finished. The news was particularly crushing for Rebekah. In addition to profound disappointment, Rebekah was also dealing with a new crack in her faith. You see, for Rebekah to do the clinical trial, a lot of specific things had to line up just right at just the right time. Well, all those things did. It's like that weird and rare time when you hit all green lights driving in the city. All the lights were green for Rebekah, and all the doors opened at the same time. She'd prayed, "Father, if this trial is not Your will, please close a door somewhere so that I can't do this." No doors closed. So we had walked through each one with confidence.

After we got the unwelcome news, a lot of pain and many tears filled several days. When the weekend rolled in, Rebekah suggested that we have a *Lord of the Rings* party. This suggestion surprised me because it's not really her type of movie. I wasn't feeling it, but I said, "Sure." I'm glad I did.

Normally, in these movies I focus in and try to identify with Aragorn, the rogue warrior, heir to the throne, who is also insecure and full of doubt. Besides that, he's a total badass. The hobbits are cool, but kind of boring compared to Aragorn and his warrior companions. But this time Aragorn was not my focus. As I watched with Rebekah, we both identified with the two hobbits, Frodo Baggins and Samwise Gamgee.

The ring came to Frodo, and it became an awful burden. He didn't ask for it and never sought it out. Someone or something else chose him to carry it. In the first movie, after a long grueling journey of running, hiding, fighting, and lots of death, Frodo said with tears in his eyes, "I wish the ring had never come to me. I wish none of this had happened."

Then Gandalf, the wizard, spoke into his mind: "So do all who live to see such times, but that is not for them to decide. All you have to decide is what to do with the time that is given to you."[16] What timely words for Rebekah and me....

Then, at the end of an intense battle in the second movie, *The Two Towers,* Frodo again feels the awful weight of the ring. It is trying to take over his mind, and in a state of confusion, he had almost cut Sam's throat with his sword. Frodo falls back and, in despair, says, "I can't do this, Sam." Rebekah and I often feel that same way, so both of us were gripped by the emotion of this scene. Then Sam gets up and says this:

> "I know. It's all wrong. By rights we shouldn't even be here. But we are. It's like in the great stories, Mr. Frodo. The ones that really mattered. Full of darkness and danger they were. And sometimes you didn't want to know the end because how could the end be happy? How could the world go back to how it was when so much bad had happened? But in the end, it's only a passing thing, a shadow. Even darkness must pass. A new day will come, and when the

---

16 https://www.youtube.com/watch?v=pjAAC13al9s Look up: The Lord of the Rings - All you have to decide (Gandalf) quote.

sun shines, it'll shine out the clearer. Those are the stories that stay with you, that meant something even if you were too small to understand why. But I think, Mr. Frodo, I do understand and know now. The folk in those stories had lots of chances of turning back only they didn't. They kept going, because they were holding on to something."

"What are we holding on to, Sam?" Frodo asks.

"That there's some good in this world, Mr. Frodo, and it's worth fighting for."[17]

Tears filled both Rebekah's eyes and mine. Sam and Frodo— they were us! And both of us knew that Someone was speaking to us about our "ring." We are too small to understand all the details, all the whys, but like Sam, we do know that something bigger is going on, something far greater than we can see with our eyes. You and I—and everyone else on the planet—are cast in a story that at times we don't want to be in, that at times we hate and want to run away from. But something bigger is going on than our immediate feelings.

AN EPIC HOPE

The characters in *The Lord of The Rings* realized that they were in a Great Story. In *Searching for God in the Lord of the Rings,* Kurt Bruner and Jim Ware share this observation:

> One of the most charming aspects of Tolkien's mythic realm is that, though clearly fictional, it has the feel of a time and region that were once real, possibly long forgotten parts of our own ancient history. This is no accident. Its creator went to great lengths to shape a fantasy world that consistently reflects those realities that frame the story in

17 https://www.youtube.com/watch?v=k6C8SX0mWP0 Look up: LOTR The Two Towers - The Tales That Really Mattered…

which men of all ages have lived. As a Christian, Tolkien understood that our lives are part of a grand drama that both transcends and explains our experiences. The drama's narrative infuses meaning into scenes and events that would otherwise seem arbitrary and meaningless. Tolkien saw the adventure of our lives, like the adventure of his hobbits, as part of a story that began "once upon a time" and is moving toward its eventual "ever after."... Their story is our story: a compelling picture of the epic drama playing out on the stage of time and eternity.[18]

That is what keeps us going. That is why I could never lose total hope. The secret that I knew—and continue to rest on—is that I am part of a Grand Narrative unfolding on the stage of time and eternity. Of course I don't know how that narrative is going to play out, nor do I always like it as it does, but I can have confidence that the Story is not just ultimately good—which it is—but that it's also good for me.

But I only know these things if something else is true. I'll explain. The truth that God's plans for me are good is all pie-in-the-sky unless God is there. I mean, *really* there. And really here now. If there is no God, then life has zero meaning or purpose, and thus hope is nothing more than wishful thinking. Oh, we may try to create meaning and find purpose for our lives other than loving and serving God, but all our creative efforts have just relative meaning, little made-up meanings, not ultimate meaning. But because God *is* there—*is* here—then everything else is here and is happening for a reason, a meaning, and a purpose.

But even then, God is basically irrelevant unless He communicates with us. Remember that whole thing about *propositional*

---

18 Kurt Bruner and Jim Ware, *Finding God in the Lord of the Rings* (Carol Stream, IL: Tyndale House, 2001), xi–xii.

revelation? Yeah, God needs to speak to and communicate with His creation if we are to know anything at all.

Well, Rebekah and I believe that God has done exactly that, that He has spoken to us about Himself. Put simply, Rebekah and I are Christians. We believe the Bible is God's special revelation of Himself and of His eternal plan. And, as the Bible itself says, *The Word of God is living and powerful* (Hebrews 4:12). The Bible gives us *specifics,* it gives us *truth,* and it gives us *knowledge* about reality because its Author is the Creator and Sustainer of all reality. In addition to providing us with a distinct worldview, the Bible tells us *where* we are, *who* we are, *what* the problem is, and *what* the solution is. The Bible also says that God is working out His great *eternal plan* (Ephesians 3:11). To Rebekah and me, God says, *There is surely a future hope for you, and your hope will not be cut off* (Proverbs 23:18) and *"I know the plans I have for you, declares the* Lord, *they are plans for good and not for evil, to give you a future and a hope"* (Jeremiah 29:11).[19] That is Rebekah's EPIC Hope and mine.

Simply put, Rebekah and I believe that a great Author stands behind all reality, all of which He spoke into existence. We also believe that He is constantly sustaining everything and guiding history according to His Grand Narrative. We believe we are characters in this Great Drama, and our lives are little stories integral to the Grand Story. Our lives have chapters that open and close, that come and go. And as Samwise says, the stories that matter—the ones that people remember, the ones that make a difference—are the stories filled with trials, struggle, enemies, and learning to overcome with faith, hope, and love. Those are the stories that matter. Thus even our struggles, our failures,

---

19 I understand this verse was originally written for Israel. But I also believe that all who are in Christ (i.e. Messiah) are partakers of God's promises and blessings made to Israel, including the simple yet hope-filled-fact that there is a God who has a good plan for my life.

and our tragedies have meaning. They are not—they are *never*—without purpose. We may not understand why something happens and we may not like it, but because that chapter is part of something far bigger, something ultimately even good, we can continue to push forward and fight. We can continue to hope.

In the next chapter, we'll look at some distinctive features of this EPIC Hope. In what ways does it differ from Mundane, Moderate, and Mega hopes? What makes this *another kind of hope* so special? We're finally getting to the coolest stuff, and I can't wait to share it with you! Let's go!

CHAPTER 10

FEATURES OF AN EPIC HOPE

WHEN I WAS in my teens and throughout my twenties, I don't remember fearing much of anything. I lived with a happy-go-lucky, naïve, and youthful bliss. Around the time I hit 30, that changed. I guess I woke up to life in the actual world where actual monsters lurk both without and within.

When my life plans did not come to fruition the way I'd wanted them to, when the wheels of life started falling off, when my own heart betrayed me and tried to destroy me, and when God didn't rush in to rescue me every time I needed to be rescued, I started realizing that this world can be a dangerous place. Life is not safe. Sometimes even God did not feel safe. As I write this, I'm now 42, and I realize more than ever that trying to navigate life is risky business. When you wake up, open your eyes, and pay attention—when you really care about people—life can be freakin' scary.

> 'Tis a fearful thing to love what death can touch.
> A fearful thing to love, to hope, to dream, to be.
> — JUDAH HALEVI (12TH CENTURY)

At times I tend toward despair. I think that comes from the philosopher/artist in me: I can be kinda dramatic. I'm a dreamer and a visionary: yes, my head's in the clouds a lot. I think about worldviews. I agonize over the meaning and purpose of life. I wonder why we're here, why there's so much evil and suffering, and why we struggle. I even wonder, *Why is there something rather than nothing?* Like I said, kinda dramatic.

But sometimes I just don't get life—and I don't even get my own self. Sometimes I just don't think I'll make it. I try and try and try to the point that I'm ready to throw in the towel. I feel like a salmon swimming upstream in life, and the effort to keep going can get exhausting. Despair slimes in.

WHAT COMPELS ME ONWARD

But something compels me to keep going, to keep pushing forward, to keep hoping. And it's not some vague desire or hope that things just have to get better. What keeps me going is something specific and real. It's some very specific things that I know. It's a very specific Person whom I know. It's the true and living God. But what does knowing Him mean? Lots of people say they believe in God or in a Higher Power of sorts. What's different about my God? What's the big deal?

I'm so glad you asked. Okay, it all boils down to that word *revelation*.[20] Remember? God has spoken, and He's revealed to us things about Himself. God's revelation is not exhaustive, but what He has revealed is true. Why wouldn't it be? I mean, if there is a God and He speaks to us but lies to us, well, we're all royally

---

20 Two questions often arise as to *How do you know that the Bible is in fact God's revelation?* and *How do you know that the Bible is accurate and has not changed over time?* These are good and necessary questions, but they are beyond the scope and purpose of this book. Questions like these are part of the special province of the field called *apologetics*, a field that's been my passion for the past 20 years. These types of questions are easily and convincingly answered when one has both the time and the willingness to listen. The list of recommended reading at the end of this book offers resources that address these issues.

screwed. So, let's assume here that God has spoken to us, and these words are true. You game?

I want to share with you three distinctive aspects of God that He has revealed to us. These three characteristics, especially when seen together, not only make this God highly unique but also provide the only grounds for a real, unbreakable, EPIC Hope. In fact, these three truths distinguish God from any other world religion, philosophy, or human conception of god—and I find that uber exciting. For me, it's not dry theology; for me, it's life.

1. **GOD IS KNOWABLE.** This fact may not seem like a big deal to many people, but many people's brains are asleep. This truth is downright astonishing! Millions of people say they believe in God or some kind of Higher Power, but they don't *know* God. Whatever god is to them, he/she/it is not a distinct and knowable person. Their god is impersonal. It doesn't speak to them or reveal anything specific. It's just there... doing what? Who knows!

    The late philosopher and theologian, Francis Schaeffer says, "Let us notice that no word is as meaningless as is the word 'god.'" He explains:

    "Of itself it means nothing. Like any other word, it is only a linguistic symbol—g-o-d—until content is put into it. This is especially so for the word 'god,' because no other word has been used to convey such absolutely opposite meanings. The mere use of the word 'god' proves nothing. You must put content into it. The word 'god' as such is no answer to the philosophic problem of existence, but the Judeo-Christian content to the word 'God' as given in the Old and New Testaments does meet the need for what exists—the existence of the universe in its complexity and of man as man. And what is that content? It relates to an infinite-personal God, who is personal unity in diversity on the high order of trinity."[21]

This one true God is a real and distinct Person. He has a personality, a nature, specific attributes, and a will. Now, you wouldn't like it if everyone around you made up things about you and, with their words, painted a detailed picture about you that isn't true, would you? Imagine these imaginary people creating a fake Facebook page with your name and picture, but all the details are false. Imagine if there were hundreds of these fake pages about you. They're completely contrary to who you really are as a person. I'd be furious if that happened to me. So would you.

Yet this is exactly what scores of people do with God. Rather than humbly recognizing our place in creation (to be specific, *we* are the creation!) and acknowledging what the Creator has told us about Himself, we project onto God what we think He should be like or what we want Him to be like. But you yourself want people to come to you without preconceived ideas, to listen to you with an open-minded willingness to truly know you, and to, as a result, get an accurate view of who you really are,

---

21 Francis A. Schaeffer, *He Is There and He Is Not Silent* (Wheaton, Illinois: Tyndale House Publishers, 1972), 13-14.

right? We need to extend this same courtesy to the true and living God.

The true and living God is a real and distinct Person who has revealed Himself to us. Now, because God is infinite and we are finite creatures, we can never fully understand God. That's a given. But this reality doesn't mean that we can't know anything about God. We may never be able to know Him exhaustively, but we can know truths about who God is because He has revealed those truths. And I think this is pretty darn cool.

But let's take this further. There's an essential difference between knowing facts *about* God and *knowing God*. We can know a lot of things about God, but not know Him just like I can know a lot of things about the president, but that doesn't mean that I know him—or, more to the point, that he knows me!

In the Bible God says that people should not gloat or boast about their own wisdom or their own power, but they should gloat and boast about knowing Him (Jeremiah 9:23-24). On the eve of His death, Jesus prayed to God the Father that all believers would *know* Him (John 17:3; also 1 John 2:13).

But here is the super uber cool part: This God wants to know us! The Creator wants to have a living relationship with us! You can't know or have a relationship with a force, with a Universal Intelligence, or with some nebulous cranky old Man Upstairs. Relationships happen only between distinct persons.

So, the first awesome aspect of an EPIC Hope is that God, the Creator of all that exists, is knowable as a Person. This reality is remarkable among all the world's religions and spiritual philosophies.

2. **GOD IS TRANSCENDENT.** I love this! Don't let that word scare you. It's packed with life-changing significance. That God is **transcendent** means that He is outside the reality we perceive. God exists outside our time/space continuum. God existed before He created reality, and He exists independent of it.

God created everything *ex nihilo:* "out of nothing." By sheer will and fiat, God spoke all reality—seen and unseen—into existence. And God sustains and upholds all things by His powerful word (Hebrews 1:3). By His will alone do all things exist and continue to exist (Revelation 4:11).

So, God's transcendence means that He is *independent* of His creation. Why is that important for hope? It's crucial!

This transcendent aspect of God is largely what I'm referring to when I talk about *another kind of hope.* As we've seen, all people have Mundane, Moderate, and Mega hopes. But all these hopes are only personal wishing, wanting, or desiring. We also call it "positive thinking."

Remember that these kinds of hope are also completely subjective. They are self-manufactured. They all start and end in our minds. They are contained there. That's how our minds work; that's how we live and survive. The problem is, we find in

ourselves little to no power to change the course of
the future, to find comfort, or to experience relief
from fear, worry, pain, and suffering. But what if
there is another kind of hope not bound by those
restraints? What if another kind of hope is avail-
able that doesn't come from our own minds, but
comes to us from outside our minds? What if
another kind of hope comes to us from outside
time and space all together?

That *another kind of hope* exists in the transcendent God whom the Bible describes as a *living
hope* (1 Peter 1:3). Read that phrase again: a *living
hope.* Not an impersonal force. Not a vague Higher
Power. But a distinct and knowable Person, who
lives and dwells eternally, apart from finite time
and space, who governs history, and who can meet
us on our level with His love. That is the kind of
hope we need because this kind of hope can actually do something. This kind of hope can change
the future and give us comfort and peace. This
living hope pierces our finite reality from outside
time and space, reaches down to us, and trans-
forms our hearts and minds.

Nearly all of the world's religions and spiritual
philosophies that are popular today offer nothing
like this. Instead, nearly all other belief systems
teach some form of **pantheism**. The Greek word *pan*
means "all" or "every," and *pantheism* is the idea
that everything, the entire universe, is God or part of
God. Twenty-first-century pantheism comes in many
forms, and although people will put a lot of spin

on each one, all those forms reduce God to a finite being or force that is equal to the universe. In pantheism God is not outside and independent of creation; God *is* the creation and therefore He changes with it as it changes, meaning He is subject to it.

This idea has many bleak implications. Consider: if "God" *is* the universe or part of it, then no distinct and knowable Person of God exists. No *another kind of hope*, no EPIC Hope, exists, and we are stuck with only self-manufactured well-wishing.

Do you see why I am so thankful, so stoked by the God of the Bible, by the true and living God who is a distinct Person, eternal, unchanging, existing outside and independent of the universe, a God who can invade time and space with His limitless power and love? That God be transcendent is a crucial and necessary feature toward having an EPIC Hope, the kind of hope that we really need.

3. **GOD IS IMMANENT.** The word *immanent* means "remaining in": God remains *in* and always remains *active* in His creation. One scholar put it this way: "The God of the Bible is no abstract deity removed from, and uninterested in his creation. The Bible is the story of God's involvement with his creation, and particularly the people in it."[22] I love this truth! God is not so far removed, not so beyond us, not so transcendent that He has no care, concern, or involvement in our lives. No, God actively involves Himself in the lives of ordinary

---

22 Wayne Grudem, *Systematic Theology* (Grand Rapids, MI: Zondervan Academic, 1994), 267.

people like you and me. From the Bible's first pages, God walks and talks with His people. To those who know God, He is not only above them; He is also *with* them and *in* them (Ephesians 4:6).

The **apostle Peter**, who knew Jesus and walked with Him for three years, later wrote to the early Christians who were suffering horrible persecution, and he encouraged them to cast all their cares and anxieties on God *because He cares for yo*u (1 Peter 5:7). Did you catch that? God—the all-powerful, almighty, transcendent Creator of the universe— cares for you. Crazy. Amazing. Awesome.

This truth that God is immanent is significant because it counters an old and inaccurate view of God called *deism*. First appearing in the 17th and 18th centuries, deism was an attempt to answer new philosophical challenges to the Bible. Deism says that God is there, but that He (it?) is so transcendent that He is not at all involved in the world. Yes, God created the universe, but then He basically walked away. Deists think of God as a divine clockmaker who wound up the clock in the beginning and since then has just let it wind down on its own.

Deism is still alive and well today. Whenever people say they believe in God, but they don't follow the Bible, or when people say they believe in a Higher Power or the Man Upstairs, or even when people say they believe in an Intelligent Designer— all these people are affirming deism. This god doesn't interfere with creation by **providence**, miracles, revelation, or **incarnation**. The god of deism is an absent slumlord who is too weak to help or too uncaring to intervene. Either way, this god is practically useless.

WHAT'S THIS ALL MEAN?

The teaching that God is immanent is not unique to Judeo-Christianity. Many ancient religions have immanent deities: the gods of the Greco-Roman era, the millions of gods of Hinduism, the divinities of Native American animism, and the popular views of pantheism in our own day (we use the term *New Age*) reside within created reality as part of it. All such gods and deities are therefore finite—limited and localized—and, like us, subject to the ever-changing fabric of our time/space continuum.

Result: *No transcendence = no grand narrative... and no EPIC Hope*

The teaching that God is transcendent is also not unique to Judeo-Christianity. Islam, for example, teaches that God—Allah—is wholly transcendent. In fact, Allah is so far above and beyond created reality that he does not interact with his people on a personal level. As such, practitioners of Islam have no *relationship* with Allah. Furthermore, Allah did not so love the world that he sacrificed himself or his son (he doesn't have any sons) for those who follow him. Allah is not knowable in a relational sense because he is so transcendent.

Result: *No immanence = no fulfillment of The Big Five... and no real Hope.*

Here's where things get atomic. You see, Christians know the Grand Narrative and understand The Big Five because they know God, the God of the Bible who is both transcendent and immanent. In other words, God is *infinite* and *personal*. Consider what theologian Wayne Grudem says about this God:

> He is infinite in that He is not subject to any of the limitations of humanity, or of creation in general. He is far greater than everything He has made, far greater than anything else that exists. But He is also personal: He interacts with us as a person... We can pray to Him, worship Him, obey Him, and love Him, and He can speak to us, rejoice in us, and love us.[23]

No other system of theology, no other religion, and no other philosophy of spirituality has a God who is both infinite and personal (or transcendent and immanent). Those gods may be one or the other, but not both. And for us to have real, objective hope—to have a Grand EPIC Hope—we need a God who is both infinite and personal. Schaeffer says,

> "There is no other sufficient philosophical answer... You can search through university philosophy, underground philosophy, filling station philosophy—it does not matter which—there is no other sufficient philosophical answer to existence... There is only one philosophy, one religion, that fills this need in all the world's thought, whether the East, the West, the ancient, the modern, the new, the old. Only one fills the philosophical need of existence, of being, and it is the Judeo-Christian God—not just an abstract concept, but rather that this God is really there. He really exists."[24]

God's transcendence ensures that our hope is objective: it exists outside our subjective minds, and it is not self-manufactured wishing. God's transcendence also assures us that hope

---

23 Ibid, 167.
24 Schaeffer, *He Is There and He Is Not Silent* (Wheaton, Illinois: Tyndale House Publishers, 1972), 13.

resides outside of created (finite) reality and that this eternal God has an eternal plan, a Grand Narrative, that He is actively unrolling.

Result: *An objective Grand Narrative... and a real EPIC Hope.* See Illustration 2.

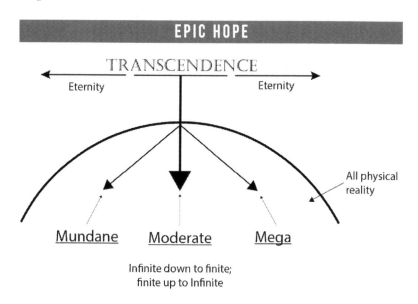

Infinite down to finite;
finite up to Infinite

God's immanence ensures that this transcendent God is intimately involved in our life. He cares for us. He loves us. God is personal and knowable, and He actively invades our world and our lives to speak to us, to guide us, to teach us, to help us, to save us, and to comfort us in the deepest place of our hearts.

Result: *Fulfillment of The Big Five... and real hope.* See Illustration 3.

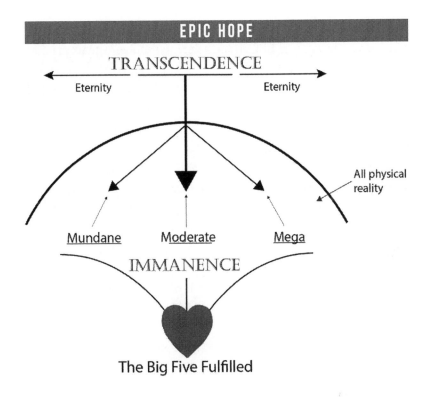

God's transcendence meets our need for an objective, absolute, unbreakable hope that does not rely on our subjective selves. But that in itself is not enough. It's definitely amazing, but if that's all we have, we might as well all become deists or even atheists. I'll explain why.

God's immanence—the reality that He is here with us—meets our subjective need for propositional revelation from God. We know from the Bible that we are not alone, that God hears us when we talk to Him, that we can have a relationship with Him, that our lives have meaning and purpose, and that His Spirit dwells in those who believe. We also are able to know a peace and comfort that surpass human understanding. In short, God's immanence satisfies The Big Five needs that every human heart has.

Together, we have the infinite personal God, the Creator of heaven and earth. The Bible often refers to God as "the living and true God." I love that.

So what keeps me going every day? What has pulled me out of the depths of drunken depression and despair? Why have I not ended my life? Because of *what I know and Who I know.* These truths about God are some of the "certain things" that I know. These truths won't leave me alone; these truths nag at my heart and chase after me when I run from them. These truths are powerful and transformative.

Furthermore, I can't give up on life because God is here with me even in my brokenness, my despair, my rebellion, and my sin. God is here, and He is love. I'm part of something eternally big, a Grand Narrative of EPIC proportions. This EPIC Hope both transcends life's circumstances and fills my heart.

"Okay. Great, Joel," some people may still object. "I see what you're saying. But so what! You know certain things about God, but how does that change anything? What difference does any of this make in your life? It's not like knowing all this fixes all your problems. It's not like God swoops in and rescues you from all the struggle and pain of life. God didn't save you and your family from the pain of divorce. God hasn't healed your wife of cancer yet. What difference does all this really make?"

Legit. I get it. I've asked these questions myself many times. And at times I still do. I don't know all the answers. I don't think I ever will. But I haven't shared with you in this chapter all that I know. There's more. In fact, what I shared with you in this chapter only scratches the surface of some super amazing truths. The ideas I shared in this chapter lay the foundation and present the necessary conditions needed for real hope, for what I call EPIC Hope. But keep reading. In chapters 12-17, I'm going to do my best to answer these tough questions, and I'll share with you what practical difference all this makes in my own life.

But before I do that, we—you and I—need to have a serious talk. We need to deal with the big ol' elephant in the room. He's been here a long time, and it's time we deal with him head-on. This elephant, though, is more about you than it is about me. Feeling nervous? Good. No more pussyfooting. Let's go.

PART **THREE**

HOW TO KNOW REAL **HOPE**

CHAPTER 11

ETERNITY ENTERS TIME

THIS IS THE most important chapter in this book. Some of you will love this chapter. Others of you will read it with curious suspicion. And I know that for some of you, your bookmark will find its eternal resting place at some point of this chapter.

Up until now, much of what I've talked about is hypothetical, abstract, and philosophical. Now, though, we will see a collision of theory and history, of eternity and time. And you will see the most amazing merger in history.

A JEWISH ELEPHANT

This book is about hope. Real hope. It's not about knitting or raising cats or growing your business. It's about hope, and hope really is an issue of life and death. You can know everything, you can believe everything I've shared so far, yet still find yourself lost, without purpose, without hope. And the elephant in the room quietly nods his head in agreement. He's been here the whole time. He's amazingly patient. This book would be a failure and I, a fraud, if I didn't introduce the two of you.

His name is Jesus.

Jesus. Those two syllables make many people get angry or

roll their eyes, but in both cases, the real issue is, they're afraid. Down deep, that name evokes something. I find it so interesting and so telling that our culture is afraid of the name *Jesus*. No other name elicits such reactions. You can talk about Buddha, Gandhi, Mohammed, Allah, Joseph Smith (Mormonism), Pope Whoever, the Man Upstairs, a Higher Power, the Force, or a Universal Intelligence, and no one cares. Really: No. One. Cares. Good for you that you found something that helps you. But mention Jesus? Either people want to run and hide, or their fangs and claws spring out like Wolverine's.

Want proof? Schools, businesses, hospitals, and various organizations will bring in, allow, and promote many Eastern Religions, **New Age spiritualism**, even Islam. But talk about Jesus or the Bible, and you'll find yourself in an H.R. hot seat. That happened to me. Years ago I worked at a Fortune 500 software company. Almost in passing I mentioned something about Jesus to a twenty-something coworker. She—and her purple hair—immediately ran and cried to H.R. that my words offended her, yet she often blabbed about her lesbian sexcapades. The next day I was in the manager's office along with the company's H.R. rep. They hemmed and hawed, wrung their shaky hands, and debated whether I should be fired or only written up. They were more afraid than I was! I received a stern warning and a write-up.

There's something in that name. *Jesus.*
Jesus Christ.

THE DANGEROUS JESUS

Whoa! That *Christ* thing—that's the biggie. That's what does it for people. But why? It's because the word *Christ* is as much about us as it is about Him. All those other religious founders and leaders are like cardboard cutouts, powerless objects of interest and study. We look at them, but they don't look back at us. That's not how the Christ is—and people somehow know it. Deep in our hearts, all of us know it. We feel it. And... we don't like it. He not only looks back at us, but He looks deep within us. Jesus controls the game, and we don't like that. We study tidbits about Jesus, but He knows *everything* about us. When we look at Jesus, we see who we really are when we see, in contrast to Him, who we aren't.

And that angers us and terrifies us.

To avoid God and self-confrontation, we keep ourselves distracted—by TV, phones, social media, busyness, other belief systems, etc. Furthermore, we are all masters of denial—of pain, emptiness, anger, fear, addictions, and the things we think and do that violate our conscience. We each have a public self and a private self. All other religions and religious figures deal largely with that public self, with the outward show. Oh, some religions encourage deep reflection and introspection, but it's about *you* looking inside *you* at *you*. But the Christ pierces our private world, our heart of hearts, and those places where we hide (Psalm 51:6; 1 Samuel 16:7).

The Christ speaks to us in the deep and calls for us to face Him. He invites us to come out of denial, and we respond with kicking and screaming. I'm no different. Facing Him leads me to face the real me inside—and the thought horrifies me. Getting even that first glimpse of Christ starts the earthquake that shatters our little kingdoms.

But here's the thing. Here's the kicker. Here's what we all know. A glimpse of Jesus wouldn't horrify us if He weren't who He claims to be. This getting to know Jesus wouldn't terrify us if God didn't exist and if Jesus were a fraud. Our popular culture wouldn't move heaven and earth to excise Jesus if He were not *the* Christ. And the culture wants to excise the Christ because He is as much about *us* as He is about His assignment on this earth, at least in the beginning when we recognize how far short of His standards we fall. But let's go deeper.

Even if we knew God existed, but He or it was merely the Higher Power that people like to talk about, the god of deism, we wouldn't care much: *Okay, cool. There's a Creator of sorts, so at least we know that life is not one big cosmic crapshoot. Now, let's cruise over to Taco Bell and get some double-decker tacos* (love those). That would pretty much be the extent of the response. *God?* Cool. *Tacos?* Mmm, even cooler. *Tacos, burritos, and a new season of my favorite show on Netflix?* Later, God.

That kind of disregard and dismissal works with every other world religion and spiritual philosophy, but not with Christ. Why? Well, I think it's His ability to look back at us, look deep within us, and speak to our hearts. It's also this thing about Him called *perfection.* Yep, I just went there.

Think about it. If there were no absolute standard of right and wrong, of good and evil, Jesus could look in every cupboard of my heart, and I wouldn't care. Sure, there's dirt. Sure, there're some spiders, some slime, some broken shelves, but broken by whose standards? Life is working for me. I'm getting by... sort of. If no universal, absolute standard of morality existed, I wouldn't be bothered by this Christ peering into my heart. My conscience wouldn't yell at me when I violate that standard. I wouldn't hide my secret deeds and thoughts. More to the point, I wouldn't hide them from myself instead of facing them. (Do you think animals deal with all this? Nope. They just *are.*)

The Christ and the God of the Bible bother us so much, not because of the call to face ourselves, but because we are to face ourselves in light of His holy standards. We are to recognize Him as God and ourselves as His creation. There lies the rub.

OH, NO . . . I'M IN TROUBLE

When I was a teenager—and that was before I was a Christian—I assumed that God and I were cool. He did His thing, and I did my thing. It worked well for me that way. As I've shared, in my late teens, I was a punk and a hoodlum, racist and mean, but I was cool with God. Or so I thought. And one reason I thought so was because I could find plenty of people who were far worse than me. Hey, I hung out with people worse than me. I also figured that if God's going to get anyone, surely He'd start with the Hitlers of the world, then move down the line to serial killers, then one-off murderers, then kidnappers, rapists, drug dealers, carjackers... You get the idea. I was darn good compared to *those* people.

But then a close friend of mine—a hoodlum turned Christian—started showing me who Jesus is, and something happened in my heart. That's when I realized, *Oh, crap. I'm in trouble.* The whole time I had been comparing myself to people worse than me to justify myself before God. I was evaluating myself by *my* standards, my subjective and **relative standards**. But when I came to God—the living and true God—on His terms, I learned that God doesn't compare us to other people; God compares us to Himself. And that freaks people the heck out. So people and popular culture avoid Jesus Christ like the plague.

So, because Jesus is everything we aren't, yet God expects us to be as He is, He is and always will be the trillion-ton elephant in the room.

My former-hoodlum friend, though, helped me see that when

I compared myself to a holy and perfect God, I melted. I was toast. I was history. I would, literally, be going to **hell**.

Then, when I finally got honest with myself, I realized I wasn't even neutral about God; I was *against* Him. My indifference, my hiding, and my attempt to make God in my image pitted me against Him. Jesus Himself said as much. While on earth, He clearly said that if you're not *for* Him, you are *against* Him (see Matthew 12:30). There is no neutrality when it comes to our attitude toward God and Jesus.

What can we do? Who can live up to such a standard? We're screwed. We're titanically screwed if we choose one of the only two possible reactions to the reality of a holy God.

The first reaction that leaves us realizing we're screwed is the popular one, the easy one. It's when people hear whatever they hear about the Christ and say, "Screw this! I don't want to deal with any of this stuff." They run, hide, ignore, deny, reconfigure, rewrite, and/or fight. They pretend that they don't know the truth about themselves, that they don't recognize God's holiness, and that all this God stuff just isn't true. These people continue to seek meaning, purpose, and hope in all the common gods that fail. I'm not here to judge this reaction. Again, I get it.

The other reaction, however, is the complete opposite. Rather than hardening their heart, the people who hear and recognize God's call experience a melting. Their tight grip of control over their life loosens. They stop seeing themselves as god and start seeing themselves as God's creation. Responding with humility, they ask God—with utter sincerity—"What can I do? What do You want from me? How can I be right with You? How can I know You?"

Sometimes we don't hear and recognize God's call, until reality crashes down around us. We no longer have the option of living distracted and in denial. Life forces us to sober up and grow up.

You see, our initial understanding of who the living and true God is, is not always comforting. God is holy and perfect, and I am not. (I'm definitely not!) And since God is both just and holy, He can't simply sweep our unholiness and evil under the rug. Doing so would not be just; that action would go against His nature, which is an impossibility. We all know that justice demands lawbreakers be punished. Hold that thought.

In order for me—or you—to "be right with God," as my dad said to me during his last days, we must be perfect and sinless ourselves. Another impossibility! Makes sense that some people say, "Forget that. I'll do my own thing and hope it all works out somehow."

But what if there is a way for God to see us as holy and perfect? Sound like pie in the sky? Too good to be true? Sometimes, honestly, the truth about God definitely seems to me too good to be true. But that, my friend, is the utter beauty of Christianity. And we call this astounding beauty *the **gospel**, the Good News.* I'll explain what this *really* means soon.

Now to the greatest merger in human history that I mentioned earlier. What I'm about to show you—this merger—is the *focal point* of all history!

In the previous two chapters, I've talked a lot about God and the ideas of *transcendence* and *immanence*. What if transcendence and immanence *merged*? What if transcendence and immanence came together in one *Human Being*?

ETERNITY MERGES WITH TIME

In the Bible, God reveals to us that transcendence and immanence merged in the man Jesus. God the Son, both infinite and personal, became flesh and lived among us. The Bible refers to Jesus as "the Word," and the Word *is* God. This is one reason why Christians get so crazy happy about this Jesus guy: He *is* the eternal God. The **apostle John** penned possibly the most astounding sentence ever when he wrote, *The Word became flesh and dwelt among us* (John 1:14).[25]

There it is. There's the merger. The Word (eternal transcendence) became flesh (temporal immanence).[26] Christians call this event the *incarnation*. The Word became flesh. *God* became a *man*. Jesus is God *with* us (Matthew 1:23).

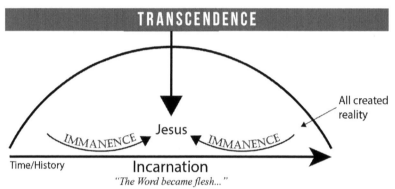

"The Word became flesh..."

But why? Why in the world would this perfect God do this? Because of *Who* He is. Because not only is God holy, righteous, and just, but He is *equally* love, **grace**, and **mercy**. At the exact right time in His plan, God sent forth His Son as the ultimate

---

25 John chapter 1:1-5 and verse 14 is one of the Bible's many references to the Trinitarian nature of God. There is *one God* who exists eternally as *three distinct Persons:* the Father, the Son, and the Holy Spirit. If that's a new idea to you, don't worry about trying to figure it all out right now. For a clear explanation and undeniable discussion of God's Trinitarian nature revealed in the Bible, start with *The Forgotten Trinity* by James R. White and then *The Trinity* by Robert A. Morey.

26 The Bible and Judeo-Christianity are distinct among the world religions and spiritual philosophies that are nothing more than speculative theology, abstract ideas, and homespun moral teachings. The distinction is that Judeo-Christianity is rooted in verifiable history. One latecomer to the game that claims to be historical revelation is the Book of Mormon (1830). It talks about entire empires, civilizations, peoples, monies, wars, and more, but it has zero—zero—archaeological support or confirmation. In contrast, archaeology and ancient historians have confirmed the vast majority of historical accounts recorded in Scripture. See for example *The Stones Cry Out* by Randall Price, *Archaeology and Bible History* by Joseph P. Free and Howard F. Vos, *The New Evidence That Demands a Verdict* by Josh McDowell, and many more.

solution to our deepest problem, to our need for a bridge between a holy God and sinful us.

Jesus is God *coming down* to us. Jesus shows us—on our level—who God is and what His heart is like. John Calvin said that God "condescends" to come down to our level and speak to us as a nurse speaks to a newborn baby.

Amazing.

THE EMPATHIZING JESUS

Jesus lived on this earth for 33 years. He knows what it's like. He's not some transcendent wholly other God who can't relate or empathize with us. He knows what we experience because He has experienced it too. He faced temptation as we do, but He never gave in. Jesus lived a joy-filled life here, but He also felt anger, sorrow, and fear just as we do. He suffered. Oh, did Jesus suffer. He knows how it feels to be misunderstood, rejected, and even betrayed. He knows the pain of false accusations, slander, and mockery. He knows physical pain and cruel torture. Jesus knows the pain of being flogged and crucified by evil men. If *anyone* knows what you're going through or how you're suffering, that Person is Jesus.

Jesus was not some mild-mannered Jewish hippie roaming around kissing babies, handing out bread, and giving good moral advice. The religious leaders of His day killed Him. Brutally.

Why was He murdered?

SIMULTANEOUS PERSPECTIVES

The Jewish leaders murdered Jesus for two reasons, one human and one divine. On the human level, Jesus died because He really pissed them off. Jesus claimed to be the **Messiah**—the Christ, the long-awaited, long-prophesied Savior of God's people. This claim threatened the power that the Jewish leaders held and enjoyed. Oh, and Jesus also claimed to be God. The Jewish leadership felt bloodthirsty rage at this proclamation, and through deceit and manipulation, these leaders framed Jesus with false charges punishable by death under Roman law.

But something much bigger was going on behind the scenes. Remember that whole Grand Narrative thing I talked about before? The eternal God had a bigger plan, an eternal plan, that He carried out in this Jewish-Roman-Jesus drama. The apostle John put it this way: *God so loved the world that He gave His one and only Son, that whoever believes in Him shall not perish but have eternal life* (John 3:16). God sent Jesus into this world to save lost and broken people (hint: that's everyone!) from the consequences of their sin. To do that, Jesus had to die.

In fact, hundreds of years before Christ's birth, the Old Testament prophets foretold that the Messiah must die (see Isaiah 53, for example). Jesus was *foreordained...* before the foundation of the world... by the *predetermined plan of God...* to come to earth and die (1 Peter 1:23; Acts 2:23; 4:27-28).

Sounds crazy, huh? God had planned Christ's death, and Jesus had agreed to that plan. Why? That seems counterproductive. Jesus could have, like Gandhi, started a revolution and changed history. Why did God prevent that and instead kill the Christ? Well, three statements will help you understand God's purpose.

First, God did not send Jesus to earth just to give us new moral teachings. Jesus offered us some profound teachings on life, yet much of it was not new. He didn't invent some new religion called Christianity. Jesus was a Jew, a rabbi, and He followed and upheld every jot and tittle of the Jewish Old Testament. He Himself said, *"Do not think that I came to destroy the Law or the Prophets. I did not come to destroy, but to fulfill"* (Matthew

5:17). But much more important than *what* Jesus said is *who* Jesus is. **C. S. Lewis** put it this way:

> I am trying here to prevent anyone saying the really foolish thing that people often say about Him: I'm ready to accept Jesus as a great moral teacher, but I don't accept his claim to be God. That is the one thing we must not say. A man who was merely a man and said the sort of things Jesus said would not be a great moral teacher. He would either be a lunatic—on the level with the man who says he is a poached egg—or else he would be the Devil of Hell. You must make your choice. Either this man was, and is, the Son of God, or else a madman or something worse. You can shut him up for a fool, you can spit at him and kill him as a demon, or you can fall at his feet and call him Lord and God, but let us not come with any patronizing non-sense about his being a great human teacher. He has not left that open to us. He did not intend to.[27]

Second, our problem is far worse than any new teachings, any new information, can solve. God reveals that we have corrupt hearts and minds. It's that word *sin*. We do what we know is wrong. We are lawbreakers. We are guilty—and I don't mean just that we have guilty feelings. I mean we all have an objective *legal* and *moral guilt* before God. We have a bad record in heaven (legally) and a bad heart on earth (morally). This objective guilt requires real justice. Someone has to settle the account and pay the debt incurred by the broken laws. Think about it like this: God didn't deal with our guilt by giving Jesus community ser-vice hours and probation. Our **sin** required that Jesus—the Son of God—die. In order for God to accept us—again, as my dad

---

27 C. S. Lewis, *Mere Christianity* (London: Collins, 1952) pp. 54-56.

said, in order for us "to be right with God"—our guilt required a reckoning. Someone's gotta pay.

Third, I ended chapter 7 saying that God seemed to have a colossal problem: *How can God—who is both just and merciful—exact justice but pardon wrongdoing and evil? How can God satisfy justice by punishing evil yet at the same time forgive the guilty and let them go free?*

The solution: *God so loved the world, that He sent His one and only Son.*

God is not only the Judge; God is also the Savior. And God is love.

Furthermore, our transcendent God has an eternal plan, a Grand Narrative. According to that plan, the Word became flesh in Jesus, and He took His people's place as God judged their sin... and that judgment was death. You see, God doesn't just say He loves us; He *showed* us when He sent His Son to take on Himself the punishment for our sins and to die (Romans 5:8).

On a human level, Jesus of Nazareth was crucified: He was nailed to a cross where He would suffer an excruciating death by asphyxiation. Evil men put this sinless Man to death. But, on a divine level, God Himself was also putting Christ to death. On the human level, a Man died. But on the divine level, behind the scenes, what was really happening in that Man's death?

Answer: God *judged* sin by judging Christ. God the Father poured out His wrath on His Son. Jesus is the Lamb of God who takes away the sin of the world (John 1:29). While Jesus hung on the cross, God turned His back on His beloved Son, prompting Jesus the Man to cry out, *"My God, my God, why have You forsaken Me?"* (Matthew 27:46). On the human level, darkness fell over the land. On the divine level, Jesus bore upon Himself the full weight of God's wrath against sin. Right before

He died, Jesus said one word: *Tetelestai*, which translates *"It is finished."* Jesus was the sacrifice for our sin that God provided on our behalf. The Bible calls this event *the **atonement**,* an Old Testament word and concept. Jesus atoned for—He paid for—the sins of His people with a sacrifice, with the perfect once-for-all sacrifice, with the sacrifice of Himself.

By judging Christ, God solved the problem He seemed to have: How can a just and merciful God enforce justice but mercifully let guilty lawbreakers go? Paul explained the atonement of Christ this way: God can *be just **and** the justifier of the one who has faith in Jesus* (Romans 3:26). There it is. Jesus paid the price, so now God can freely offer pardon—He can grant total forgiveness—to anyone who has faith in Jesus.

As you probably know, a dead Christ hanging on a Roman cross is not the end of the story. His followers wrapped His body in ceremonial cloth, placed Him in a tomb, and rolled a massive boulder in front of the entrance. Three days later, as prophesied in the Old Testament and as foretold by Jesus Himself, God resurrected the corpse of Christ. The resurrected, living Jesus showed the world that, in His death, God had received payment for sin, and then God showed His power over death. Again, this good news about Jesus paying for our sin and us receiving His forgiveness is what the Bible and Christians call *the Gospel.*

GOD'S OFFER

God wants to know us, and He has made a way for us to do exactly that. We can know Him, participate in His Grand Narrative on this earth, and then live with Him forever. And I can't think of anything better than that, can you? I mean, for real, if all this is true, can you think of anything greater than this?

Okay, so how do you get onboard? How does a person make

this happen? What do you have to do? Here's the short of it: believe that Jesus is God's sinless Son whom God sent to pay for your sin. That's it. Salvation is a gift. You don't do anything to receive it. You don't earn it by now trying to be really good, and you wouldn't even gain salvation if you were able to completely stop sinning. Salvation is not about anything you do or don't do. Your salvation is all about what Christ did—and not at all about what you do. That's the utter, uber, amazing, crazy good news of Christianity!

When you put your trust in the true and living God, when you believe in Christ for your salvation from punishment for your sins, God forgives you of all your sin—past, present, future. He then lets Christ's perfect record apply to your account, so to speak. That and that alone—God's act of grace, of giving you something you don't deserve and can't earn—is why a person can be sinless in God's sight. That is how a person is—to use a Bible word—**saved**. That is why we can know God. To try any other way to gain God's acceptance and forgiveness will not only be futile, but the effort would be to deny God's distinct and holy Personhood, to ignore our own moral guilt, and to proclaim that Jesus' death was unnecessary.

Christ's perfect righteousness credited to us takes care of our bad record, of our—so to speak—criminal record in heaven. God now regards us, His kids, as being sinless just as Jesus is. And when we believe in what Jesus accomplished on the cross, God sends His Spirit to dwell within us and give us a new heart. The presence of the Spirit helps us in real time with our still morally bad heart here on earth.

We started this chapter with an enormous elephant in the room. No disrespect intended, but that elephant had a name: Jesus. The Christ. And you either love that name, or you hate it. There is no middle ground. Oh, many people say they aren't Christians, so they don't pay much attention to Jesus. But remember, like that young me, the "Jesus" they have no issue with is not the historical Jesus we meet in the Bible, the Man who claimed to be—and, in fact, was—God incarnate, the Man whom the Romans nailed to a wooden cross on a hill called Golgotha. The "Jesus" whom people choose to ignore actually looks more like them than the Jesus from history. This Jesus I have introduced you to, *this* Name—you will either love it or hate it.

When we first come face-to-face with this Jesus—this Christ who looks back at us and deep into our souls—this Jesus is frightening. We want to hide from this Jesus. But once we realize how much this Jesus loves us, the fear will fade. When we realize to what extreme lengths God went to build a bridge between Him and us, that remarkable love should melt our hearts. This once-terrifying name of Jesus then becomes the most precious name ever to be spoken. God is not out to get us; He is out to rescue us from eternal punishment, from eternal separation from Him. That's why Jesus came to earth!

Understandably, we may still deal with the fear of letting Jesus into every area of our life. That, too, should melt when we realize that God is gracious—He gives us what we don't deserve—and merciful—He doesn't give us what we do deserve. Both His grace and mercy reveal the truth that God loves us more than we will ever really know!

When the real Jesus enters our life, He brings comfort, peace, power, courage, love, and faith to our hearts. He also brings another kind of hope: Jesus brings eternal and EPIC Hope.

I love the name of Jesus because I love Jesus. He's my Christ, my Savior. He's my Friend and my Lord. He's my King and my

Brother. He's my God. Transcendence and immanence merged in Jesus who is our living EPIC Hope.

The Word became flesh and dwelt among us.

CHAPTER 12

HOW THIS TRUTH CHANGES EVERYTHING

YESTERDAY EVENING, WHILE driving south on the 57 (that's a freeway in SoCal), I could feel a new heaviness enter the air. Rebekah and I were heading home, tired, excited to slip into some cozy clothes and crash into bed with our abused but beloved companions: Netflix and Prime. A woman from church was bringing us dinner. Meatloaf was all we'd been told, but we were so hungry that a loaf of fluffy meat sounded like a royal meal to us.

Two weeks before that, Rebekah and I had found out that the clinical trial she was doing for her brain tumors was not working. In fact, we also learned that new tumors had sprouted up and the old ones were growing. Five weeks ago, there were two; now there were seven.

All the doctors and all the researchers had been so excited and hopeful that this new treatment could be the answer, the cure. (This is definitely Mega hope stuff.) Rebekah, normally full of faith and hope, took the news hard. It was a crushing blow, and for the first time since I've known her, she questioned God's goodness. For the first time ever, I saw a crack in the armor of her faith.

But when the clinical trial stopped, her doctors created an alternative plan: they would do targeted brain radiation. So, for the third time, Rebekah's having radiation on her brain. Yesterday was the first of five straight days of radiation. For radiation, technicians first create a special plastic mask fitted to her head and face. Only her eyes and nose show. On radiation day, Rebekah lies on a cold metal table. The techs put the mask over her face and bolt it down to the table like some medieval torture device. The room is all white and cold. After she's bolted down, the techs exit the room, and the metal table slides into a monster machine. Behind safety glass, the techs and doctors, all in white coats, push buttons, twist knobs, and click mice. They were aligning the radiation lasers with pinpoint precision.

Rebekah lay alone in the cold white room, head bolted to the metal table, feet sticking out of the monster machine's mouth. Before the techs scuttled out of the room, they asked her what music she'd like to listen to. There are little speakers by her head, and the techs can play YouTube music into them. Rebekah told them, "Micah Tyler." The music started, and the monster came to life. For 45 minutes, she lay eerily still while the monster spit its radiation lasers into her brain. At one point, she told me, a tech came in and wiped a tear from her eye. Apparently, a camera is on her face, but she never saw any camera....

The hospital is an hour from our house, so we have a lot of drive time. On the way home yesterday, without Rebekah saying a word, I felt it. We were fine for a while, talking about random things, but after a couple minutes of silence, I felt it. I felt the heaviness in her heart.

"What is it, babe? What's getting you?" I asked gently.

After at least a minute of thick silence, she said in a small, shaky voice, "When I was in there, I was listening to the music, and I was praying. I was feeling so scared. I'm not ready to die...."

(In moments like this, I just shut up and listen.)

She continued: "I was feeling so afraid over all this, but as I listened to the words of the song and prayed, suddenly I felt God there with me. He was right there in the room with me. And a peace came over me. I'm not done. I don't know how to explain it, but I'm not done doing what I'm supposed to do here. I don't know exactly what that is, but I know that it's not my time yet."

"You're right, babe. Each one of us is immortal until God says it's time."

"Yeah. I just knew He was there with me, and that made all the difference."

THE WEAPONS OF OUR WARFARE

Knowing God is not like having a magic shield that keeps struggles, failures, pain, and suffering out of your life, and knowing God is not a quick fix or automatic deliverance from tough circumstances and difficult situations. This truth makes many people wonder, *Then what difference does knowing God really make?* Here's the quick—clichéd—answer: it makes all the difference in the world. The final five chapters will go deeper than the cliché and highlight some key differences that knowing God makes in a person's life.

I've chosen five truths that, for me, are the most powerful. These truths serve as powerful weapons when the battle of despair rages in our hearts. The Bible uses the word *heart* holistically to represent our entire self: our mind, our emotions, our beliefs, and our will. In this sense of the word, then, the battle for life or death, hope or despair, lives in our hearts. That is the principal battleground for what is primarily a spiritual fight.

I'm not saying that we don't use normal human means to

fight against despair and pain. If you have cancer, you fight with proven treatments like chemotherapy, radiation, surgery, and immunotherapy. If you suffer from depression, you might fight with prescribed medications. If you battle PTSD, you might fight with medications, therapy, and/or support groups. If you've lost an important relationship or a loved one, you might rely on family, friends, community, and therapy for support as you fight. All of these connections are good, and all are powerful. Rebekah and I rely on all these sources of help and healing.

After all, we human beings are far more than mere biological bags of stuff that another person or a pill can fix. Our secular culture likes to think that way because that's all they have! Without God, there is no EPIC Hope, so a pill or a professional is all they've got. But at our core, we human beings are far more than just matter-in-motion responding to various stimuli. At our core, we are spiritual beings created in the **image of God,** and the actual battle for hope is invisible. The site of the battle is the heart: it's you against you. We fight against that voice that whispers to us in the night, that seductive voice that says, *You won't make it.... This is too much for you.... You're not strong enough.... Life will never be normal again.... You'll never feel happy again.... You're a failure... Give up on this lost cause.... You're going to die soon. You might as well end it now.*

I've heard each of those voices countless times. (That list came from my head!) So how exactly do we fight that!? I'll tell you: we fight using the powerful weapons of truth God has given us. These weapons offer another kind of hope, a hope that—you may know how I'm going to finish this sentence—makes all the difference. And this hope that can uniquely *comfort* our heart-of-hearts and *compel* us to keep fighting, to keep trying, and to keep getting up no matter how many times we fall. Let's jump in.

CHAPTER 13

EPIC HOPE #1:
I AM NOT ALONE

WHAT COMPELS ME to keep going when life sucks? Truth. Those "certain things" that I know. These truths compel me to keep pushing forward when I struggle, when I'm afraid, when I fail, and even when I directly rebel against God. But it's more than just surviving. Knowing these "certain things" helps me thrive and find deep joy in life however intense the battle. As Sam said to Frodo, "There's some good in this world, Mr. Frodo, and it's worth fighting for."

I'M NOT ALONE

At first glance, this difference that God is making in my life may not seem so spectacular. But follow me here, and you'll see that it's titanic on two fronts.

First, popular philosophy and culture promote various forms of **secular humanism** and **atheism**. They say there is no God who created the universe or who exercises **sovereign** rule over the course of history—and He's especially not managing my life! These people believe instead that the universe essentially created itself, that it came into existence as the result of blind chance and accident. They don't believe in a **supernatural** realm. Everything that exists is matter and energy in motion, controlled by the impersonal laws of nature, or by chance, or by whatever you think. And—their thinking continues—as humans, we are basically nothing more than complex material and chemical cocktails animated by internal and external stimuli. And when we die, our bodies dissolve and melt back into the natural elements from which we are made. We completely cease to exist. There is no **soul** and no afterlife. No, at death, they say, you—and those you love—are one... hundred... percent *erased*—forever. You're done. *Forgotten.*

How exciting, right? Give me a break! And we wonder why the US has such a high rate of depression, anxiety, suicide, and the use of psychotropic drugs. Also, many people will talk about whatever form of secular humanism or atheism they adhere to, but they can't consistently practice what they preach. They will always smuggle in elements and concepts of Christian theism to make life both livable and sensible. That we are just some big cosmic accident, that Planet Earth is nothing more than a speck of dust floating aimlessly through the cosmos, and that death means the complete extinction of our conscious self—these thoughts are painfully depressing and downright terrifying when you meditate on them and come to really understand them.

So what does EPIC Hope #1 have to say? First, we see that God's existence makes a massive difference in a person's life. The shift from atheism to theism is a monumental change of worldview. But mere theism—simply acknowledging that God exists—is still severely limited, which brings us to the second titanic aspect of this hope.

"Okay," many will still say, "God exists. What's the big deal?" This is the general feeling of the average person on the street who holds to some form of deism or even pantheism. For them, god is a nameless, faceless, impersonal force or a Higher Power. I'm sure that god is important—or at least he/she/it was important in the beginning to get everything started. But for daily life and issues, this average person finds this he/she/it god is irrelevant: "Oh, God's cool and all, but I'm hungry for some Taco Bell."[28] And I would agree. I'm always up for Taco Bell. But I digress. So if all we know of this god is, he/she/it is *there*... Seriously, what's the big deal? Double-decker tacos are more exciting than that!

But that idea of god in general is radically different from the God revealed in **Scripture**. The Bible teaches us that God is a distinct personality. He is actively involved in His creation. He is present at all points of this world at all times. He reveals Himself and speaks to us in various ways, such as through creation itself, through our own image-bearing conscience, through His people, and especially through His inspired Word. Yes, God is here, and He is *not* silent.[29]

When we believe in the true and living God whom we meet in the Bible—and holding that belief means we also believe in the Person and the atoning work of Jesus—God adopts us into His family. With this adoption, this once distant, even frightening Creator becomes our Father (Ephesians 2:19), and God calls us His beloved children (1 John 3:1).

When we know the Christ, we know God. Jesus is *Immanuel*, a word that means "God with us." But there's more. Not only is God *with* me, His child, but my Father God is *for* me. God's on my side, He's in my corner, and He has my back. If you have

---

28 I realize I reference Taco Bell a lot. I don't eat it that often, but it is one of my favorite food groups.
29 *He Is There and He Is Not Silent* (1972) is the title of a little book by the late theologian and philosopher Francis A. Schaeffer (1912-1984). Actually, it's the third book in a trilogy, preceded by *The God Who Is There* and *Escape from Reason*. I was introduced to Schaeffer's works when I was 21, and they changed the course of my life. The other person who blew my mind open to a whole new way of thinking and seeing reality was the late Greg L. Bahnsen (1948-1995). I recommend the works of these two men for anyone who wants to strengthen the intellectual side of their faith.

kids, think about how much you love them. Think about—better yet, *feel*—how much crazy passion you have for them. Feel how committed you are to rooting for them and fighting for them. God feels the same way about His children, only infinitely more so. Our Father is not against us; He is for us (Romans 8:31-32).

Would you believe that life gets even better in yet another way when we know God? According to Scripture, God is not only *with* me and *for* me, but He also dwells *within* me (1 Corinthians 3:16). Can you get more intimate than that? This connection between God and His kids is so intimate that God gives us permission to call Him *Abba* (Romans 8:15-16). The word *Abba* is an Aramaic term that's similar to our word *Daddy*. It's a word of personal intimacy. This biblical picture of God is a far cry from regarding Him as some distant, nebulous force!

Knowing these truths about God can bring us tremendous power and a deep sense of comfort. Our friends or a spouse can come alongside us and bring a degree of comfort. For some of us, our parents can also bring comfort. (There are just times in life when, no matter how old we are, we need our mommy or daddy.) But spouse, parents, and friends can bring us only a limited amount of comfort. In the end, I'm left alone with myself and my thoughts. No human can reach the deep places, my heart, my soul.

So think for a moment about lying awake at night, being by yourself in a hospital room, or lying—alone—on the radiation table. At times like that, it's only you and you alone—unless you know the living God as your Father. But if you know God as your Father, then you *know* He is right there with you, and sometimes you feel His presence. God your Father has the power to calm the raging waters of your anxious heart. You can cast all your fears and concerns on Him, leave all that with Him, and trust that whatever happens, He's there, and He's got you. You will also know *the peace of God, which transcends all understanding, and will guard your hearts and your minds in Christ Jesus* (Philippians 4:7).

Did you notice the word *transcends* in that last sentence? Yep, same word and concept we talked about earlier. God is never anxious, worried, or afraid. God is always at perfect peace, and He willingly shares that peace with us. God's peace does *transcend* all human understanding. Jesus can and does give us a supernatural peace that calms us when circumstances should freak us out. This peace we experience defies human rationality (Isaiah 26:3). King David said it like this: *Even when walking through the dark valley of death I will not be afraid, for You are close beside me, guarding, guiding all the way* (Psalm 23:4 TLB).

Here's my last thought on this wondrous truth: that I am not alone and that God is always *with* me and *for* me doesn't mean that I'll always have this supernatural peace, nor does it mean that God will magically rescue me from all my troubles. We've seen that. Life in this world is proof enough. But what my knowing God does mean is that no matter what I face in this broken world and in my frail body, He will be with me in a way that no human being can. All of us will go through dark valleys and deep waters, but hear this promise from your Father God:

> *"When you go through deep waters and great trouble,*
> **I will be with you.**
> *When you go through rivers of difficulty,*
> **you will not drown!**
> *When you walk through the fire of oppression,*
> **you will not be burned up—**
> *the flames will not consume you." (Isaiah 43:2)*

When I'm in those fires of life, I can keep going because *He Himself has said, "I will never leave you nor forsake you"* (Hebrews 13:5).

When I was in my twenties, I believed all of this, but my belief was largely theoretical. After the wheels of life fell off, this truth became oxygen and blood, absolutely life giving and life sustaining.

So maybe at first glance, the truth that God is with us may not seem too spectacular. But when we understand it, as God reveals it in His Word, and as we experience it for ourselves, this truth of His presence is more than spectacular. It is transformative. And it is my next breath.

CHAPTER 14

EPIC HOPE #2: LIFE HAS MEANING

I've talked about this idea in chapter 8 and elsewhere in the book, but I return to it again because this powerful concept fuels a hope that will persevere. Knowing that I'm part of God's Grand Narrative—His EPIC Story of the ages—is the primary idea that kept me going after my divorce and after my umpteenth time of failing to stay sober.

About a year after my divorce, still lost and struggling, I had some friends from church invite me to move into their house to regroup and rebuild. I wasn't doing well at my dad's. John and Stacey had a sizeable house, no kids, and a couple unused rooms. I spent about five months there. Every morning we had breakfast together, spent some time together reading and discussing God's Word, and talked about life. Then I helped them pull, pack, and ship products. (John and Stacey owned a small home-based business selling stuff on Etsy. It amazed me that they could make such a good living selling beads online.) My kids spent the weekends there with us, and we all had a splendid time. It was super chill, safe, and exactly what I needed. I also spent a lot of time thinking and journaling.

John and Stacey lived in the boonies, in what people called "cow country." There were lots of farms, and the entire area smelled like manure. After about a week, you didn't notice it anymore. I often took lengthy walks through cow country, walking for miles and miles, always carrying a spiral notebook with me. I walked and talked with the Lord. During my time with my friends in cow country, I filled seven notebooks with my thoughts, with insights about life, about myself, and about healing. This idea of the Grand Narrative is one of the main thoughts sprinkled throughout those journals. I remember feeling like an explorer who had discovered a whole new continent for the first time, and this Grand Narrative thrilled me. It provided a context to help me make some sense of the past. It also gave me strength and hope for the future. And even some excitement.

A GRAND NARRATIVE IS IN PLAY

God has a grand and eternal plan for this world. His intention is twofold: *to display His glory* in every way, but primarily through the death and **resurrection** of His Son and, by Jesus' death on the cross for our sins, *to make possible our salvation and adoption*, gifts that provide our deepest joy and contentment. John Piper says it like this: "God is most glorified in us when we are most satisfied in Him."

As He carries out His Grand Plan, God is in absolute control of everything. This upsets many people, even professing Christians. Yet what are the alternatives for what's happening in this world—in our life—and *why*? Well, from a secular worldview, the alternative is blind chance, and if that's the case, then we have no basis for meaning, purpose, morality, inductive reason, knowledge, science... or hope.

The other alternative I see is a theistic worldview, even a

Christian one, where God limits His control and allows humans **autonomous** control—complete independence—over the shape of the present and the course of the future. While this seems like a nice option, it ultimately reduces God to a finite and therefore limited god who doesn't know the future (he is not omniscient) and who is severely limited in power (he is not omnipotent). I'm reluctant to hope in a god like that. (I know, heady stuff and discussions for another book.[30])

Let's see what God says. First, in the Old Testament, we read these words of God:

> ***This plan of mine is not what you would work out,*** *neither are my thoughts the same as yours! For just as the heavens are higher than the earth, so are my ways higher than yours, and my thoughts than yours.*
> *As the rain and snow come down from heaven and stay upon the ground to water the earth, and cause the grain to grow and to produce seed for the farmer and bread for the hungry, so also is my Word. I send it out, and it always produces fruit.* ***It shall accomplish all I want it to and prosper everywhere I send it.*** (Isaiah 55:8-11 TLB)

This passage comforts me because plenty of times I don't understand God's plan, and—frankly—sometimes I don't even like it. It's not what I would do—and God isn't surprised by that! *"This plan of mine is not what you would work out,"* He has said. Honestly, we shouldn't expect to understand all the plans and workings of an infinite God. If we could understand all God does and why, He wouldn't be a very big God.

---

30 For further study on the secular dilemma, see the works of Francis A. Schaeffer and *Pushing the Antithesis* by Greg L. Bahnsen (Atlanta, GA: American Vision, 2007). Bahnsen also has hundreds of downloadable audio lectures. For further study on the theistic dilemma, see *No Place for Sovereignty* by R. K. McGregor Wright (Carol Stream, IL: InterVarsity Press, 1996). For an excellent little book on God's sovereignty, see *Evangelism and the Sovereignty of God* by J. I. Packer (Carol Stream, IL: InterVarsity Press, 1961).

Now let's look at a **New Testament** passage. The **apostle Paul** is speaking to a group of Greek philosophers in Athens. They've put him center stage, in the very same place that, hundreds of years earlier, the philosopher Plato sat when he was on trial. Paul said this:

> *The God who made the world and everything in it is the Lord of heaven and earth and does not live in temples built by human hands. And He is not served by human hands, as if He needed anything. Rather, He Himself gives everyone life and breath and everything else. From one man He made all the nations, that they should inhabit the whole earth; and He marked out their appointed times in history and the boundaries of their lands. God did this so that they would seek Him and perhaps reach out for Him and find Him, though He is not far from any one of us. For in Him we live and move and have our being.* (Acts 17:24-28 NIV)

Sounds to me like God is in control! We also see in Paul's words the transcendence of God the Creator *and* the immanence of God who *is not far from any one of us*. This idea of a sovereign God controlling everything can lead to terror and despair if we fail to understand some revelations about God's nature. For example, *God is love* (1 John 4:8), and He proved His astounding love for us in the death of His Son (Romans 5:8; John 3:16). The Bible also reveals that God is all good. God is also all knowing (omniscient). There is nothing in all created reality that God doesn't know (1 John 3:20; Psalm 139). He even knows our inner thoughts and feelings (Hebrews 4:12-13; John 2:24-25).

God is all powerful (omnipotent) as well as all loving, all good, and all knowing. When we hold these truths about God together, we can trust His plan even when it makes little sense to us. As Job said, *Though He slay me, yet will I **trust** Him* (Job 13:14). Other translations say, *Though He slay me, I will **hope** in Him*. *Trust* and *hope* are used interchangeably because they are two sides of the same coin. Trusting in God is to hope in God; hoping in God is to trust God. Without putting our trust in God, we have no hope. But when we understand God's character by faith, we can continue in hope.

When we see a well-rounded picture of God, passages like Romans 8:28 not only make sense, but bring deep comfort: *We know that in all things God works for the good of those who love Him, who have been called according to His purpose.*

SEEING LIFE AS A STORY

So, when I was staying at John and Stacey's house, I was thinking about all this stuff a lot. I started seeing my entire life as a story that is part of God's Grand Story. Like all stories, my life had had many chapters, some exciting, some tragic, many seemingly mundane. My choices and desires are real and significant, but I'm not the ultimate author of my story. I'm the hero of my story, but I'm not the major hero of the overall story.

I'm not alone in this big ol' world, and my choices are not brute **existential** leaps of faith devoid of meaning and purpose. I don't create my own meaning, purpose, significance, and value. Rather, because and only because I'm part of the Grand Narrative and created in the Author's image, I already have tremendous meaning, purpose, significance, and value, so much so that the Author of the Great Story of time and eternity sent His one and only Son to die for me!

Like chapters in a book, the chapters in my life open, and they close. Always. If we don't recognize these openings and closings in real time, we see them when we look back. Often, a chapter in our life closes because of a loss. New chapters open when something new or exciting happens or when we replace what we lost in the previous chapter. All noble stories—the ones worth reading, as Samwise said—are the ones filled with villains and danger, struggle and perseverance.

I started seeing my own life like that. I mean, I really saw everything through this new lens. I realized that I want to live a noble story, one that is significant, one that impacts this world. God knows that's my heart. As much as we might dream of winning the lotto, quitting our jobs, and relaxing in self-indulgent pleasure for the rest of our lives—as awesome as that story may sometimes sound—in reality, that story totally sucks. No one would ever want to see or read that story. It's a story no one can relate to. It would be a waste of paper.

As I was thinking through all this, I started seeing my life as an adventure rather than a bummer. Sure, I'm not an Aragorn, a self-doubting ranger fighting the evil forces of Mordor, trying to save Middle Earth, and hoping to reclaim his rightful throne of Gondor. I'm not Frodo on a journey through peril and terror, trying to destroy an evil ring by throwing it into the lava of Mount Doom. I'm also not Neo fighting against the Matrix to save humanity from a kajillion self-aware machines.

WE *ARE* TRUE STORIES

No, I'm just me. You're just you. But you know what we *are* that those other characters are *not*? We are *real*. I think I will make a t-shirt that says, "Your Life Is a True Story."[31] We are true stories!

Now think about how our stories are part of the Grand Story,

---

31 "Rebekah loved the idea of this shirt, so we made it! It reads "I'm A True Story." You can check it out and get one for yourself at www.rebekahshope.com" (FYI – we have two domains for Rebekah's Hope. The main site is .org but we also own the .com for it. The .com goes to our clothing store).

the Story written by an omnipotent, eternal Creator about a beautiful world gone awry, warrior angels and foul demons, a long-awaited promise of redemption, a virgin giving birth to a Savior who is the Son of God, the unexpected death of that Savior, His surprising resurrection from the dead and ascension into heaven, a Holy Spirit descending back to indwell and empower those who follow the Savior, a fight against sin and evil, an archenemy named Satan trying to destroy the Savior's followers, and a mission where eternal heaven or hell hang in the balance for the world. Yep, that's *my* story! I hope it's yours too.

I started seeing this true story—my story—as an adventure. Chapters open and close, but the end of a chapter is not the end of the story. Oh, it may *feel* like it, but the story continues unless I selfishly and foolishly choose to close my book or unless God inks the last period and calls me home.

And check this out. Unlike Aragorn, Frodo, Neo, Harry Potter, William Wallace (*Braveheart*), Alice stuck in Wonderland, or Tom Hanks's character in *Castaway*—unlike all these, we know that we are in a Grand Drama, and we know that there is an Author behind it and outside it. Think about it. We sit in the theater or at home watching these movies, caught up in these stories. At times we find ourselves on the edge of our seats, palms sweating and anxiety rising, as the character's life hangs by a thread, hope seemingly lost and defeat assured. We—like the character—see no way out. But we don't completely freak out, scream, and run for the exit. The character in the story may give up, but we don't. Why? Because we know something they don't. As viewers, we know that a very smart author is behind the story and that he or she has more to say, that this is not how the story will end. We know that, and it keeps us from losing our minds!

As we live out the true story of our life, we have the advantage

(1) of *knowing* we are part of a Grand Narrative; (2) *knowing* that there is an all-good, all-wise Author behind our story; and (3) *knowing* this Author personally. Amazing, huh? For me, it's been life changing.

LIFE *IS* A JOURNEY

I want to share with you two final applications of my understanding *and* believing that I'm part of this Grand Narrative. Remember I said that this Grand Narrative idea appeared throughout my journals? Well, a few other ideas did too. My theory is, the more fully the Grand Narrative developed in my mind and heart, the more easily I saw other subsidiary applications flow from this foundational concept.

Let me give you a little background first. You already know about the breakdown of my first family, and you know about my struggles with alcohol, with my ex, and even with God. During those years, life was confusing, overwhelming, and joyless. Fear and despair gripped my heart. Every day I heard that seductive voice whispering nasties in my head. Life was not just a confusing struggle; it was a disappointment and a bummer.

By the time I moved in with John and Stacey, I was ready for change. Defeat had held me long enough. I wanted to feel happy and start enjoying life again. I was glad to have the Grand Narrative as a lifeline, but it's also quite abstract and can still feel like cold philosophy.

So I started shifting my thinking about life. I stopped looking at my life as a series of goalposts on a timeline and began to see life as a process and a journey. What do I mean? Glad you asked.

Society conditions us to see our lives as a series of ascending steps, up, up, up, toward certain goals that we check off when we reach them. Accomplishing all that's on this list is, according to our society, the key to happiness and fulfillment. You know what I'm talking about: the way we are "supposed" to do things in order to reach the American Dream and find ultimate happiness. It goes like this: Get your college degree(s), land your dream job that will turn into a lifelong career, fall in love, get married, take fancy vacations, purchase a house, have a baby or two, trade up to a bigger house, raise brilliant-beautiful-blessed kids, get them through college, take fancy family vacations along the way, trade up to luxury cars, send out family-photo Christmas cards, purchase a cabin in the mountains for getaways, smile and laugh and look good the whole damn time, eat organic, enjoy strength and health, retire with a fat investment portfolio, volunteer at your hobby-horse charity, and, in the last scene, sit on your balcony with your spouse, sipping lattes, overlooking the city or the beach or the valley, and, with a smile, breathing in the ultimate feeling of perfect contentment and fulfillment. Heaven on earth. The perfect life. Complete satisfaction. Right?

Well, my life looked nothing like that. I tried, that's for sure. I'm not pullin' it off. Yet that ideal stands strong in our culture and in our hearts, and it can wreck us if we hold that up as the ideal—the one and only standard—of success and happiness. Unless you're just awesome (which you may be), this ideal can crush you.[32]

One Sunday when I was with John and Stacey at their church, the pastor quoted a line from a poem. It was just in passing, but the quote struck me. Back at the house, I looked up the poem. It's called *The Station* by Robert Hastings. As I read it, my heart thrilled. I saw a pathway to freedom from the tyranny of the ideal. And this path fit right in with both the Grand Narrative and the Bible's picture of the believer's life.

---

32 If the picture I painted closely resembles your life, I trust your heart is right, and I honestly commend you for all you've accomplished. Ideals are ideals because they are usually wise and worthy. My point is that, for most people, this American Dream ideal is out of reach; it's not realistic, and therefore it's dangerous.

We don't find true life by climbing the ladder and achieving each successive goal. A healthier view of life for many, if not most of us, is to see it as one long journey without a final destination this side of heaven. In *The Station,* Robert Hastings wrote, "Sooner or later we must realize there is no one station, no one place to arrive at once and for all. The true joy of life is the trip. The station is only a dream. It constantly outdistances us."

What was Dr. Hastings saying? He was reminding us that there is no one thing or goal or achievement or acquisition out there that will bring us complete peace, contentment, and satisfaction—yet that's what we constantly think! The secret this wise author taught is that there is no station! In fact, the subtitle of the book is *A Reminder to Cherish the Journey.*

The poem opens with this line: "Tucked away in our subconscious minds is an idyllic vision." And pursuit of that idyllic vision can kill us. That vision implies that happiness and fulfillment will evade us *until...* Until what? I don't know. Maybe whatever we think and believe the *it* is that follows *until.* But the secret to freedom lies in the realization that there is no *it.* There is no station. "The true joy of life is the trip." Finding freedom in this idea, I started writing in my journals "The journey *is* the destination." Read that again. Think about that. Meditate on that. Put it on notecards in your car and around your house.

The journey *is* the destination.

This statement may sound like a trendy cliché of positive thinking you'd expect to find on social media posts. To some, the idea may even sound contrary to Christianity. Isn't heaven the destination? Our time on earth is a blip on the screen compared to eternity, right?[33] Yes! Heaven is a believer's ultimate

---

33 In a great message Francis Chan uses a piece of rope to illustrate how short our earthly life is (see The Rope https://www.youtube.com/watch?v=86dsfBbZfWs). I completely agree with this teaching. I simply want to help Christians avoid devaluing the goodness of our lives here on earth.

destination, but it's not the only one. If getting us to heaven is all that God cares about, wouldn't He just snatch us up and take us there as soon as we came to faith? But He doesn't do that. And, contrary to many Christian teachers, God doesn't leave us here to use us as tools for the sole purpose of bringing other people to Christ. What I'm saying is, life on earth is important in and of itself. We're not just filling time here on earth, and it's not merely a dress rehearsal for what *really* matters.

If heaven is all that matters, why did God create this world to begin with, especially knowing how it would turn out? He did, you know. Before God created anything, He knew that His creating this world meant His Son would suffer and die. Why would He go to the extreme lengths of sending God the Son here to live, suffer, and die? God could have just started with us in heaven and avoided all the pain, suffering, evil, and death. That's what He seems to have done with the angels. Clearly, God had a different plan for us. He created *this* world, and He declared it "very good" (Genesis 1:31). At the appointed time, God the Son left the eternal and entered time and space. He took on human nature and human flesh. He died a brutal, terrible death. By creating this amazing universe and sending His only Son to this broken world to die for our sins, God confirmed that this world and our lives here are significant in and of themselves.

It's a common error in religious circles to think that our world, our bodies, and even our human desires are base, evil, and less important than what is eternal and heavenly.[34] This dualistic thinking—heavenly = good; earthly = bad—has its roots in Greek philosophy and was later carried over into medieval Roman Catholic theology in what's called the secular/sacred dichotomy. The idea divides reality into the godless secular realm comprised

---

34 I'm not dismissing or denying the doctrine of total depravity. Actually, I hold to it more than most people do. My point is, simply, our *physicality* and *finitude* are not wrong or bad.

of the common stuff on earth and the sacred godly realm comprised of the church, the Bible, priests, prayer, good works, and other things that deal with God. This dichotomy is pure fiction; it is absolutely false.

In the 1500s the Protestant **Reformation** sought to get rid of this and many other unbiblical ideas. In line with the Bible, the reformers taught that *all* of life is sacred. Pursuing studies in law, dentistry, and business is as godly as pursuing studies in theology, provided each person is doing all with God in view. A plumber can glorify God as much as a pastor or a missionary can.

Also, heaven is our ultimate destination, and it offers powerful motivation to press onward, but heaven is not to be the be-all and end-all of our life on earth. You see, God cares about our journey *now*. Furthermore, God wants us to be happy, content, and joyful in our life here on earth. A lot of religious people and Christians struggle with that idea. Of course our personal happiness is not the principal point of life, but it is a point God cares about. I confess I struggle with this idea because, at heart, I'm a works-oriented Pharisee. But if God didn't care about our personal happiness and contentment—if that's not what He wants for us—then why is the Bible filled with both commands to fight against fear, despair, depression, anxiety, and feeling downcast *and* exhortations to be joyful, loving, thankful, and content?

Life is a story. An actual story. Life is the story of a process and a journey with many ups, downs, turns, and loops. It's messy. Life is primarily a journey of the *heart* rather than a journey of *geography*. Life is primarily a journey of *awareness* rather than a journey of *acquisition*. The journey *is* the destination. This idea made me stop thinking that real life is somewhere *out there* and that once we finally attain this or that, he or she, *then* we can really start living life. No, life is *now*. Right now matters. This is it. This is life. It may get better or worse, but this is it. I'm alive *now*.

This thinking gave me permission to rest. It gave me permission to stop beating myself up. I stopped with the self-flagellation. The power of the idyllic vision of perfection subsided. I could just... be. But it was more than that. I found not only permission, but a divine exhortation to enjoy the journey. I started writing "EJ" (Enjoy the Journey) on my hand every day to remind myself that it's okay to pursue happiness. I had to remind myself to find joy in the little things—and I soon realized that those are often the things that really matter anyway.

Life will go up and down, sometimes sideways. That's a given. We can't control everything. As John Eldredge says, we need to stop the frantic arranging. We are always trying to arrange our circumstances in such a way that will recreate Eden. Eldredge's point is that we can't do it. We think we can. But we can't. So he calls us to stop all the frantic arranging.[35] There is no station. That's the secret. Understanding that is when joy and contentment can begin.

So let's enjoy the journey now. God wants us to! We'll still struggle and suffer, but the choice to enjoy the journey introduces us to fresh and life-giving freedom. As I thought about all these things, I came to a final point of life application.

LIVE NOW!

If God wants me to enjoy this journey of life, it makes sense that I do so NOW. After all, *This is the day that the* Lord *has made; we will rejoice and be glad in it* (Psalm 118:24). Today. Right

---

35 *"It can't be done.* By this I remember that I can't arrange for the life I prize. I am not fully healed yet of my addictions and my tendency—which seems so second nature—to arrange for my own little Eden now. To say again and again, 'It can't be done,' does not discourage me; quite the contrary, it frees my heart from the grasping and plotting and fretting over my life, which always accompany arranging. It reminds me to let it go. It breaks the power of the spell the evil one is trying to weave around us" (John Eldredge, *Desire,* Thomas Nelson Publishers, 2000 and 2007), p. 209.

now. The phrase "Live NOW!" is sprinkled throughout my seven journals. I also wrote this on my hand. "Live NOW!" is proper **existentialism**, but what's it mean? I'll get to that.

Well, you don't need me to tell you that we're living crazy, busy lives. We pack our weekly schedules with work, school, kids, sports, bills, chores, church, ministry, luncheons, meetings, budgets, duties, and responsibilities. If you're like me, you feel as though you're spinning two dozen plates all at the same time—and that's not easy! We think, *When will this craziness end? When can I put down all these plates and start living my life?! If only I had it easier... If I could just slow down... Maybe I'll get a fat raise or win the lotto...then...then I could actually slow down and start enjoying life.* Sound familiar? Well, it's how many of us think.

And all the while we're thinking those thoughts, *this* life is passing us by. This perspective is, in part, how we lose our life. We are waiting, waiting, waiting. But for what? We're waiting, waiting, waiting.... We're pacing the aisles for that elusive station. We put *Living NOW* on hold while we wait for some unknown, remote possibility to become reality. Thinking we'll get to life sometime in the future, we sleepwalk through the motions of life today. That's some background for what "Live NOW!" means.

I stumbled upon this idea to *Live NOW!* one day while I was smoking a cigarette. While I was staying with John and Stacey, I smoked. When I'd become a Christian 20 years before, I had quit smoking, and I was never tempted afterward... until. With all the marital drama and then the divorce, I picked it back up again. Smoking and drinking kinda go hand in hand.

Anyhow, I was out front of the house, sitting on the curb, puffing away. I was always thinking, thinking, thinking. Life was stable, but far from great. I didn't have a job, didn't have a home, didn't have a family. *This is it*, I thought. *This is my life.* Now, I know that sounds depressing, but it wasn't. It was the opposite because of all these thoughts about the Grand Narrative, about seeing my life as a story and seeing my life as a journey. When I muttered, "This *is* my life," it was freeing because of that perspective.

Because I saw myself as part of God's Grand Narrative and because of who God is, I am right now where God wants me to be. This… here… now… is exactly where I'm supposed to be. If I forget who God is and view Him only as a Creator, then the idea that I'm where I'm supposed to be can be a most depressing or suffocating thought, like feeling ruled and trapped by the Fates of old. But if I remember who the true and living God is—that He is all good, all wise, all loving, and all powerful—then I can trust and I can rest.

"This is it."

"This *is* my life."

"This *is* my life, right here, right now."

Although my life may not be my ideal, I can at least rest in knowing that it is God's plan for me—right now. Improvement in my situation and my own personal growth may come a week from now, or maybe a year, but right here and now, this is it. This is my life. And this is where I'm supposed to be at this point in the Story, in this chapter.

Once we understand and accept "This is my life," we can begin to find freedom from the tyranny of the Ideal; we can begin to find freedom from the lie that real living starts someday in the future; and we can begin to live our lives NOW. This acceptance means that we're not in denial, and we're not fighting ourselves, fighting others, or fighting God. We see all our negative self-talk for what it is: crap that is holding us down. Seeing our lives as part of the Grand Narrative also gives us permission to be content where we're at now. We learn to realize that such states, seasons, phases, and chapters come and go. This ebb and flow and mystery and change *is* life. This is it. *This is the day that the* LORD *has made; we will rejoice and be glad in it.*

Be glad in it. Glad? Yes! When you choose this mindset, gratitude will grow in your heart. Okay, you don't have a sweet house, don't have the Mercedes, don't have a fat retirement, don't have the hot spouse, don't have the slim body, don't have... whatever! This is it. This *is* my life. What do I have? Life! Family! Kids! Friends! Church! Water! Food! Eyes! Hands! Legs! Air! Creation! Shelter! Clothes! Transportation! Blankets! Warmth! Work! God! Eternal life! I have HOPE.

It's funny, but during those days with John and Stacey, I was practicing mindfulness before I even knew what mindfulness was, before I knew it was cool. Because I'm part of the Grand Narrative, wherever I'm at, life has meaning and purpose. Right now counts. It may not be ideal, it may be far, far, far from ideal, but right now has meaning and purpose.

We must live life as we go along. It's the only way. Because and only because we are part of God's family, in His Story, in His hands, can we truly learn to Live NOW. We can learn to enjoy the journey, to enjoy NOW. This is part of the privilege of having an EPIC Hope.

The phrase "This *is* my life" became part of my mental repertoire of truth that strengthens and protects my hope. But as I thought about all this stuff, it didn't take me long to add a qualifier:

"This is my life... and it's a good one."

CHAPTER 15

EPIC HOPE #3:
SUFFERING HAS PURPOSE

URING MY FIRST marriage, I served as an associate pastor at two churches. After a year and a half, the first church kicked me out because aspects of my theology had changed, and I no longer aligned with their espoused theology.[36] I'd felt ready to move on, so I harbored no hard feelings. In fact, I remained friends and even did ministry with that denomination.

The second church where I pastored was a great fit. The senior pastor was a renowned scholar, author, and apologist who took several of us men under his wing. While I was there, I taught classes in New Testament Greek, hermeneutics (how to interpret the Bible), evangelism, and apologetics. The senior pastor traveled a lot, and he often let me man his pulpit on Sunday mornings. It was a large church, and I thrilled at preaching the Word to this group of people I loved.

On one Sunday morning, the pastor was there in the audience listening to me preach. As a former open-air street preacher, I took that dramatic style into the pulpit and let'r rip! After the

36 If you're wondering, I moved from Arminian theology to Reformed theology.

service, people flooded up to me with praise and encouragement. Thankfully, even as a young man, I knew the dangers of such accolades. I tried my best not to take any of it to heart. I remember walking out of the sanctuary into the church foyer where the pastor was standing. Smiling, he put his arm around me as we walked toward the front door. He made some positive comments about my message, but that's not what I remember. The only words I remember him saying were his warning: "You could be the next Francis **Schaeffer**, but be careful, my boy. Your knowledge is way beyond your sanctification." Little did I know how important that warning would become.

The word *sanctification* refers to our Christian character and level of spiritual maturity. It's not that the pastor saw any dark or hidden sin in my life. It's simply that he saw me as a young kid playing with nuclear weapons. Nearing almost 70, he could see what I could not. Only a couple years after that warning, my life fell apart.

GREAT EXPECTATIONS

Trials rarely make sense while we're in the middle of them. When they pass, we try to look back to find some reasons why the hard times came, to find a purpose in them. We also try to see if any good has come out of them. Sometimes, if we're fortunate, we can find that good. Other times, there seems to be no good reason for the pain, and these are the trials that can challenge our faith. These trials prompt our strongest, most heartfelt *Why?*

Many factors contributed to my marriage and then my life falling apart, but looking back, I know the time was so confusing and so painful for me because I felt abandoned by God. In fact, I felt that God had turned against me. Looking back now at those chapters of my life, I know God hadn't turned against me, but that's how it felt while I was in the thick of it.

I think one key reason I felt so abandoned and let down was because I'd had certain expectations of God. I expected Him to work in certain ways for me, and when He didn't, nothing made sense. As I saw it, I had given God my life, and for ten straight years I gave my all to Him in devotion, in study, and in service to others. I did my part, and I expected God to do His. The problem, however, was that I defined His part; I made *Him* part of *my* plan. I had a specific plan for His role. I also expected that if I checked off all the right boxes, then He would pave a smooth road ahead for me: no major problems or struggles, a good income that paid for everything I needed and a lot of things I wanted, a happy wife, near-perfect kids, and a flourishing ministry. *I'll give my life to You, God, and I'll serve You. In turn, You give me the American Dream. Deal?* I forged God's signature on that deal.

I don't beat myself up about it. I was young and naïve. But actual trials, failure, and suffering were not part of my plan, and I'd expected I could avoid them if I played my cards right. In *Walking with God Through Pain and Suffering,* though, Timothy Keller wrote this:

> No matter what precautions we take, no matter how well we have put together a good life, no matter how hard we have worked to be healthy, wealthy, comfortable with friends and family, and successful with our career—something will inevitably ruin it. No amount of money, power, and planning can prevent bereavement, dire illness, relationship betrayal, financial disaster, or a host of other troubles from entering your life. Human life is fatally fragile and subject to forces beyond our power to manage. Life is tragic.[37]

---

37 Timothy Keller, *Walking with God Through Pain and Suffering* (Penguin Books, 2013), p. 3.

Human life is fatally fragile. Life is tragic. I've learned that—and I continue to relearn that fact. It's not an easy lesson to get our mind and heart around....

Of course we are never to seek out trials and suffering. It is good and right to work hard to avoid them, but as Keller says, no matter how well prepared we may be, life is fragile and tragic. But I've also learned that even though life may be tragic at times and even though it may even fall apart, *we don't have to.* In fact, I'm learning that more than just surviving, we can actually thrive through the hard times. Rebekah and I are living proof of that right now.

In the introduction to *Walking with God Through Pain and Suffering,* Keller shared this personal observation:

> Looking back on our lives, Kathy and I came to realize that at the heart of why people disbelieve and believe in God, of why people decline and grow in character, of how God becomes less real and more real to us—is suffering. And when we looked to the Bible to understand this deep pattern, we came to see that the great theme of the Bible itself is how God brings fullness of joy not just despite but through suffering, just as Jesus saved us not in spite of but because of what he endured on the cross. And so there is a peculiar, rich, and poignant joy that seems to come to us only through and in suffering.[38]

That's what we want to know: how to find this fullness of joy "through... suffering."[39] Notice Keller's words: "Kathy and I came to *realize that...*" and "we came to *see that...*" Much of how we progress or regress during hard times has to do not only with

---

38 Ibid., 6.

39 At this point, I will depart from Keller's treatment of the issue and offer my own insights into suffering. But if you are in the thick of suffering now and want a more in-depth study—if you want stronger medicine—I highly recommend Keller's book. If you're looking for daily medicine in a devotional style, it's hard to beat *Streams in the Desert*. Rebekah reads that every morning. We also enjoy reading and highly recommend Paul David Tripp's *New Morning Mercies*.

our perspective on God, reality, and life but also on our expectations. In the past, I had a sound theology, but it was incomplete. In part, I saw what I wanted to see, and of course I still do in many ways. But I'm always trying—or at least wanting—to learn and grow. That said, I think many people and even a lot of Christians think the way I did: I do my part, and God will do His part according to my plan. But this way of thinking makes God like a vending machine: put in your money, push a button to choose what you want, and out pops exactly that!

SEEING WITH NEW EYES

So how do we learn to find peace and even joy when we're suffering? For me, it comes down to certain things I know about God that, together, give me a fresh perspective on everything. We've looked at many of those "certain things" about God, such as His goodness, His wisdom, His power, and His care for us. We've also seen that with this God, we are never alone: He is always with us. We've learned about God's Grand Narrative, His Story that He's meticulously working out over time. And if all that we've learned about God is true, then we will—or we should—have new eyes to see struggle, failure, and suffering differently than the world sees it.

Because of who this God is, we can know that even our struggles, failures, and sufferings have meaning and purpose. I'm not saying that knowing this makes it easy, but it does ease our burdens by giving us hope that these hard times are not in vain. This hope serves as a reservoir of emotional strength that helps us continue to push forward.

Because of who this God is, we know that He *is working all things according to the good, to those who love Him, and whom He calls into His plan* (Romans 8:28). Here's the point: we may not like the particular chapter we find ourselves in, and it's not a chapter we would have planned, but it *is* part of an intelligent Plan. That's the point. Consider our culture's alternative.

The popular thinking of Western culture right now is a form of secular humanism that says the material world is all that exists or ever existed. Consequently, we are nothing more than material/chemical machines, and no Grand Narrative is in play. Instead, random accident and mere **chance** drive whatever happens. This philosophy gives no ultimate meaning, purpose, or value to anything. This view says that you only go around once in life so you might as well grab for all the gusto you can get. And especially since secular humanism does not subscribe to life after death, a person should grab a lot of gusto now!

The humanist perspective continues: Purpose and meaning are just fabrications. They're made up; it's playing pretend. Interestingly, our American Dream is a logical outgrowth of humanism: Climb that ladder of success, acquire all you can, and experience as much pleasure and freedom as possible because the sand in the top half of the hourglass is running down.

Keller offers a very different perspective: "In that [humanistic] view of things, suffering can have no meaningful part. It is a complete interruption to your life story—it cannot be a meaningful part of the story."[40] Our trials and tragedies have no meaning or purpose to begin with, so of course they can't be a meaningful part of our story. Trials and tragedies are just annoying hindrances in the pursuit of personal freedom and pleasure. It is because of this that we Americans have become so weak, so wimpy, that we experience even trivial events as traumatic.

But God's Grand Narrative provides a far more redemptive outlook. Setting the stage is the fact that we live in a fallen

---

40 Keller, 16.

world, corrupted by sin and selfishness. We are fragile creatures contending with biological, mental, and emotional limitations. Failure and suffering are inevitable, but they are not detrimental because of—you know what's coming!—"certain things" we know about God, the world, and ourselves. And as I've said before, in God's Grand Narrative even our sufferings have real meaning, purpose, and value. Our weaknesses, our failures, our struggles, our addictions, our emotional hurts, our physical pains, even our sins have value, meaning, and purpose in God's Grand Story. To me, that truth is downright awesome.

A KEY CHAPTER IN YOUR STORY

The genuine believer knows certain things, certain truths, and these truths—these revelations of reality—can generate new emotional power, grit, and even joy. When we learn to see our life as part of the Grand Narrative, we see reality with new eyes. We also see it as having supernatural and eternal significance. When we know that even our sufferings have meaning, purpose, and value, then we understand that our suffering can be crucial to our accomplishing our purpose here on earth. Our life chapters that contain suffering are not merely important; they are actually indispensable chapters in our story.

In other words, what if God designs even our struggles and sufferings to achieve something amazing for us? What if our sufferings—as counterintuitive and contrary as the possibility may seem—are actually working *for* us? Would that redemptive view of suffering change how you respond to tough times? What if I told you that the Bible teaches exactly that?

The apostle Paul knew and wrote about the value of suffering. He definitely knew hardship and suffering, both emotional and physical. This man was beaten, stoned, whipped, starved, shipwrecked, and bitten by a venomous snake as well as mocked, ridiculed, betrayed, and outcast not only by the Romans but also by his own people, by his fellow Jews. Paul wrote four of his New Testament letters from a Roman jail cell, and in the end they beheaded him because of his faith in Jesus the Messiah.

But Paul knew certain things, certain truths that not only kept him going, but even filled him with joy. For Paul, knowing the risen Christ was the greatest treasure a person can pursue. To the church in Corinth, Paul taught that when we believe truths about Jesus, *we do not lose heart* (2 Corinthians 4:16). He went on: *Though outwardly we are wasting away, yet inwardly we are being renewed day by day* (v. 16). Now check this out: *For our light and momentary troubles are achieving for us an eternal glory that far outweighs them all* (v. 17).

First, as Peter did, Paul described our troubles as *momentary*. That's similar to my saying our troubles are chapters that open and close. During our troubles, though, we easily and therefore almost always forget that the tough times won't last forever. Second, Paul said that whatever we're going through is *light* or *little*. What! Is cancer little? Is addiction little? Is mental illness little? Is poverty little? Is depression little? From an earthly perspective—from a secular humanist perspective—the answer is NO! But considering these ways of suffering from an eternal perspective and seeing God for who He really is can help to shrink our troubles. *Light and momentary* doesn't mean painless and easy, but writing under divine inspiration, Paul declared that life's troubles *are achieving for us* something very precious.

So what is that precious something? Paul referred to that prize as *an eternal glory.* And that's the eternal state of the believer, and whatever eternity looks like, it will be glorious for us. Paul once got a glimpse of this eternal state of glory, and he *heard inexpressible words, which is not lawful for a man to utter* (2 Corinthians 10:4). Greater insights about this future glory come from the apostle John in his book we call Revelation. What does the believer's future glory look like? Here's a hint: *God will wipe away every tear from their eyes; there shall be no more death, nor sorrow, nor crying. There shall be no more pain, for the former things have passed away* (Revelation 21:4). God will make all things new and glorious.

But I want you to see something else. Our troubles and sufferings not only achieve rewards for us in eternity, but they also guide us in new directions in our stories here and now—especially if our hearts are open to hearing from God.

You've likely seen this course of events in your own life. Something happens that seems terrible at the time—divorce, addiction, job loss, disease, despair—but looking back you realize that something genuinely good came out of it. Maybe you gained insights you never would have had without the trial. Perhaps you grew in strength, in purpose, in friendships, in faith, in wisdom, and such growth might never have happened apart from the tragedy.

My own life has both taught me this truth and reinforced it. I went through a brutal divorce. I struggled with alcohol, and at times I still do. I got fired from three jobs. I lost my house, I lost my ministry, and I lost my reputation. I languished in depression, anger, fear, and despair. I felt like dying at times. But now I look back, and I am grateful for all the hardship. It changed me. It helped me grow as a man. It taught me how to stand and how to get back up after I get knocked down. It gave me grit. It helped me see God and myself in new, broader, truer ways. It prompted humility. It created an empathy that I hadn't had. It taught me to find contentment in the lowest of times. It taught me that Jesus actually is all I really need in this life to be content and happy.

My trials were also building blocks that would later enable me to give back and bless others.

Had I not gone through all those hard times, for instance, I would never have met Rebekah. Had cancer never struck, our ministry to others would not exist. We'd likely just be working our jobs, trying to climb the ladders, trying to play it safe, and trying to scrape through life without getting too banged up. Most likely—and sadly—we would have lived a life of cowardly self-preservation. This book wouldn't exist. None of my books would exist. Rebekah's forthcoming book wouldn't exist. Our documentary, *A Brave Hope,* wouldn't exist. The many other hope-filled projects we have planned would never be. Instead, our story would be comprised of work, food, fun, and Netflix. Lather, rinse, repeat.

So, then, am I glad my family broke up? Am I thankful that my dad died of cancer too soon? Do Rebekah and I *want* her to keep having cancer? Are we thankful for the cancer? No, no, no, and no! Ideally, if we'd had our way, none of these tragedies and trials would occur. I'm not thankful for divorce and addiction and cancer and pain, but I am thankful that my God is with me when such troubles inevitably happen. I am thankful that my God has a Grand Plan and that He can turn tragedies into triumphs. We don't live in an ideal world; we are broken people living in a broken world with other broken people. Yet life is NOW!

Our God never promises us a bed of roses on Easy Street, but He is a God who works all things together for good (Romans 8:28). He is a God who says, *"I will repay you for the years the locusts have eaten"* (Joel 2:25). And He is a God who provides healing for the brokenhearted and those who grieve: He promises *to bestow on them a crown of beauty instead of ashes, the oil of joy instead of mourning, and a garment of praise instead of a spirit of despair* (Isaiah 61:3).

Again—because I want to be sure you get this—it's not that we're thankful for tragedies, but we do find joy in learning to see the hidden value and purpose in them and then learning how to use the pain for good. The way I see cancer, for example, is that it's here. But we give it the middle finger and try to turn the tables on it. We try to use this enemy against itself for good: "You meant to hurt us and kill us. Instead, we will use you as our tool and squeeze as much dang lemonade out of you as we can." We use this enemy against itself by finding and publicizing the hidden blessings, the beauty of the human spirit, the strength of community, the power of faith, and the love of God, all which serve as means to foster hope and healing.

Lemons are an inevitable part of life. I don't know what your lemons have been, are, or will be, but I've learned that our greatest message often results from our deepest miseries; our most effective tools for ministry and life often come from our most painful trials. The more open, honest, and vulnerable I am in my words and my writings, the more people seem to respond and be ministered to. Our challenge—your challenge and mine—is learning how to not waste our pain but to use it to make lemonade that will refresh others as well as ourselves.

We will do better at this lemon squeezing when we accept that suffering can be a crucial means of accomplishing our purpose here on earth. As I've said, our life chapters that feature suffering are not only important; they are indispensable chapters in our story.

THE PATHWAY TO PEACE

I want to end this chapter by looking at one sentence from the famous "Serenity Prayer" by Reinhold Niebuhr (1892-1971). You've probably heard the first part of this prayer.

> God, grant me the serenity
> To accept the things I cannot change;
> The courage to change the things I can;
> And the wisdom to know the difference.

In the early forties, Alcoholics Anonymous started using these four lines as their go-to prayer for support groups. I've attended many AA meetings, so I've heard this prayer recited many times. But most people don't know that this prayer has two more stanzas. Here's the entire prayer:

> God, grant me the serenity
> To accept the things I cannot change;
> The courage to change the things I can;
> And the wisdom to know the difference.
>
> Living one day at a time;
> Enjoying one moment at a time;
> Accepting hardships as the pathway to peace;
> Taking, as Jesus did, this sinful world as it is,
> Not as I would have it;
>
> Trusting that You will make all things right
> If I surrender to Your will;
> So that I may be reasonably happy in this life
> And supremely happy with You forever in the next.
> Amen.

I love this prayer. Rebekah and I have it taped on the wall in our bedroom. Those inspired lines are packed with wisdom I could rant about for an entire chapter. But, again, I only want to focus on one sentence here:

ACCEPTING HARDSHIPS AS THE PATHWAY TO PEACE.

The key idea is *accepting*—and what's the first step in most recovery programs? It's admitting that I have a problem. The purpose is to help bring us out of denial. We are good at denial because it's a way to protect ourselves. Although it poses as our friend, denial is actually working against us and hurting us. Once we come out of denial, we can then move toward acceptance, and that's where we find healing.

The only other part of the prayer where the idea of **acceptance** shows up is at the beginning: "To accept the things I cannot change." Let's pause there. Many of our trials and troubles are indeed "things I cannot change." They are issues I can't just will away. It is what it is, at least for now. To fight against such things is to be in denial about reality and thus continue to hurt ourselves and possibly others. Let me illustrate this reality with a scene from my own story.

After my divorce, one family became two. My ex-wife became the custodial parent, meaning that she had our kids most of the time. I had them on weekends and one midweek day if it worked out for everyone. So I became the weekend dad. I hated it with a heartbroken hatred. The deepest hurt of my life is losing the opportunity to be my kids' full-time dad. Knowing that this situation will hurt them—in whatever ways the impact of my not being there 24/7 manifests itself over the course of their lives—breaks my heart even more. I constantly worried about them; I still do. And living within me, somewhere below the surface, is a crushing sadness about this outcome.

At the time of the divorce, my financials kept me from giving to my kids the way I wanted to. It is what it is; it was what it was. "God, grant me the serenity to accept the things I cannot change." Initially, I raged against this outcome and harbored within myself a deep rage that burned white-hot. But doing so only hurt me and those around me, especially my kids....

As Timothy Keller said, human life is fatally fragile. Life is tragic. Hardships will happen. It's just part of the deal of being alive here. With my kids, I had to learn to accept my role as a part-time dad. I had to let go of my ideal, of God's plan for a family. I worked on accepting my new reality. I wasn't at all thankful for it, but I came to accept it, give it to God, and trust Him with it.

> *Okay, God, I'm giving my kids to You. You have a Grand Plan in play here, a plan that I believe is good. I can't control my kids' stories. They have their own journeys and their own stories, and I have mine. I'm going to let go of my anger and disappointment, accept this situation for what it is, and try to make the best of it. I'm going to learn to be the best weekend dad I can be. And I'm going to trust that You're going to bring something amazing out of all this brokenness.*

Has it been easy? Heck no. Is it easy? Again, no! And I still struggle with guilt and sorrow. But coming to a place of accepting the situation has brought peace, and this peace has freed me to focus on enjoying my kids more and moving on with my life in positive ways. It takes time and conscious effort to trust God with my kids. It takes faith....

To slightly tweak Niebuhr's wise words, accepting hardships *is* the pathway to peace.

Better: Accepting hardships as part of God's plan is the pathway to peace.

When we look at life from the perspective of the Grand Narrative, we easily accept that the enjoyable things in our lives have meaning, purpose, and value. But the coolest part of adopting the Grand Narrative perspective is that we can trust that even the hurtful things in our lives have meaning, purpose, and value. In fact, life's pain and loss can often have more meaning, purpose, and value than the enjoyable things do.

Our dark chapters become key chapters that change the course of our life—and that change us. These dark chapters also bring about new chapters filled with people and events that blow our minds in unexpected ways. Being able to trust in this redemptive ability of our God is another unique aspect of having an EPIC Hope.

CHAPTER 16

EPIC HOPE #4:
WE ARE DEEPLY LOVED

As I walked through the front door, my heart sank to my feet. The front room. Empty. I walked to the kitchen. Empty. My steps on the bare tile floors echoed in the emptiness. I walked up the stairs. The bathroom: empty. The kids' rooms: empty. "Our" room: empty. I looked inside the walk-in closet: empty except for my clothes. *It's all gone. They're all gone.*

Overwhelming pain... Too much for me to handle... I fled the house, drove to the Circle K nearby, bought some beer, some smokes, and a hotdog... and drove back to the house. That night I stayed inside the walk-in closet, drinking—numbing—until I passed out.

Waking up the next morning, my head was a mess, and the emotional pain, now intensified, hit me like lightning. I crawled out of the closet, into the middle of "our" room. On my knees, I cried. No, I bawled. I still remember the tears pouring out of my eyes. The searing pain was like nonstop electrocution. I crumpled to my knees, clawing my face, and crying out over and over, "Jesus, help me! Jesus, please help me!" One chapter had closed, and a new, dark chapter had opened. Oh God, I did *not* want that chapter to open....

We had tried several times to make things work. I hadn't touched alcohol for months up to that point. I was attending meetings and finding strength. Other factors played a role that I could not control: *God, grant me the serenity to accept the things I cannot change...*

For two years after that moment, I spiraled. Moving back to my dad's house and having lost my job as well as almost everything else, I languished. Looking back now, I see that I was desperate for connection, for intimacy, for love. I still vividly remember hearing "I don't love you anymore" and "We don't need you." That *we* was the twist of the dagger.

I share this story to make the point that, at the deepest level, hope and love often live or die together. When I felt unloved by those I loved the most, I felt not worth-less, but worth nothing. I felt that my worth as a person, a man, a husband, and a dad amounted to... zero. Now, I knew enough truth to *know* that this was false, but I *felt* like a zero. As our emotions often do, these feelings ran roughshod over my knowledge. I also felt like a burden to those I loved. *If I'm a zero and I'm a burden, what's the point of getting out of bed? God, where are You? God, You must be against me too.* It's nearly impossible to feel hope when thoughts like these fill your mind.

I had an open wound in my heart, and I didn't know how to stop the bleeding. And I couldn't put the pieces of my life back together again. But you know the one thing that did work? Getting drunk. I poured alcohol in the wound, and that took away the pain... for a moment. I also poured cigarettes, television, porn, anger, and denial into that wound. It's easy to get stuck in a place like that because these dopamine infusions seem to work. But in reality I was just adding more fuel to the fire of despair and feeling like a zero.

Yet I didn't lose all hope, as this book in your hands proves. Those "certain things" that I knew to be true kept me pushing forward. But if I'm honest, it wasn't bare truth propositions alone that birthed new seeds of hope and began new healing in my heart. Knowing certain truths is essential for hope, and that knowing kept me from throwing in the towel. But they're not what started the healing or helped me begin to feel better.

SEEDS OF HOPE

The first little seed of hope I noticed came from my kids, my four-year-old son in particular. (At the time my daughter was around 12 and struggling with her own feelings from all the chaos. Thankfully, my son was too young to catch most of it.) I always pulled myself together on the weekends when I had the kids, and I devoted my all to being present with them. But it was my little boy who poured healing oil on my heart. He was all about his daddy. To him, I was fun and strong. I was mighty. He was always in my face, always climbing on me, always... loving me. That love—unbeknownst to him—was a powerful force that planted seeds of healing and hope. I wanted desperately to be *that* dad for both my kids.

The second little seed of hope came from my parents, my dad in particular since I lived with him for about a year. Both my parents have always loved and supported me, but my dad was the one I needed most during this chapter. I know it was tough on him to see me so depressed and drinking so much, but he never stopped believing in me. At the time I knew many of my decisions disappointed him, but he also knew to give me my space and to allow a time of grieving. He told me all the time that he loved me, and whenever I made a baby step forward, he told me he was proud of me. Powerful stuff.

Looking back, I see these sources of love as bright signposts in a dark chapter of my life. Over time, baby steps started turning into big boy steps, then man steps. I learned that rather than trying to deny the pain, run from the pain, or numb the pain, I needed to let my heart bleed. I learned to live with the hurt, and the more positive steps I took forward, the more the hurt started dissipating.

Three years later, I met Rebekah, who is my sweetest (human) seed of hope. She's the biggest seed of hope because she loves me like no one else. She's an adult woman (not a four-year-old) who thinks I'm fun, smart, and strong. She believes that I'm something special. She actually thinks I'm amazing, and she tells me so! She's even seen me at my lowest. She's seen me during the times I fall and drink, and she still thinks I'm fun, smart, strong, and something special! What! Seriously? Yes. Rebekah knows me better than any human, and she still loves me like crazy. That ignites in me a vigorous confidence and power.

OUR CORE DESIRE AND NEED

These experiences I've shared all illustrate both the transforming power of love and, conversely, the destructive power of feeling unloved. Again, knowing that I'm deeply loved gives me confidence, power, and hope.

I believe that because we are humans made in the image of God, our core desire and need is to love and receive love. I believe that without loving and being loved, we will either live surface-shallow lives… or we'll wither and die. To love and receive love is the highest form of human fulfillment. All the outward successes of this world mean nothing without love. The Bible says as much: *Better is a dinner of herbs where love is, than a fatted calf with hatred* (Proverbs 15:17). The most meager meal shared with someone you love is better than a fancy feast in a mansion where everyone hates each other. No wonder God says that of the three indispensables to life—faith, hope, and love—the greatest of these is love (1 Corinthians 13:13).

While giving and receiving love from other people is our core desire and need, there's still a problem. It's not enough. It's not enough because *we* are not enough. Other people definitely plant in us seeds of love and hope, but no human can ultimately fulfill us or provide real hope. Both those tasks fall to a transcendent personal God. Likewise, no other human can satisfy The Big Five,[41] those core needs we all have, because we humans are *finite* (limited) and *sinful* (lawbreakers). When we try to find our ultimate meaning, purpose, fulfillment, and hope in another person—or, for that matter, in any finite object—we end up disappointed and disillusioned, and we destroy the other person by wearing him or her out. God didn't design us to fulfill these needs for another person. Even if we try really hard, we can't succeed.

But the problem goes deeper still. As I said, I believe our deepest core desire and need is to love and receive love. I absolutely believe this is true, but with a qualification: we desperately desire to be fully known—inside and out—and still be deeply loved. That's the challenge. While my parents know me well and Rebekah knows me quite intimately, none of them really know me completely—and they especially don't know my inner world. The truth is, if I laid out in this book everything I've done and everything in my inner world, you'd slam it shut, cast it from you as though it were suddenly on fire, and then pray for my salvation—and probably call the cops.

---

41 To recap The Big Five, we want to know the following: (1) we are not alone; (2) life has meaning; (3) suffering has purpose; (4) we can find the power needed to get us through Mega storms; and (5) there is life after death. The Big Five are listed and briefly defined in Appendix 1.

While that's kind of funny, it's way too close to the truth. When Paul took an honest look at his own heart, he cried out, *Oh wretched man that I am! Who will deliver me from this body of death?* (Romans 7:24). And if we're honest, you and I are no different!

God and God alone knows each one of us thoroughly—the good, the bad, and the ugly. This truth, though, is not always comforting. When you read the beginning of Psalm 139, David seems distressed about having this kind of God. I get the sense he wanted to run and hide from this all-knowing, all-seeing God who is perfect and holy. But by the end of the psalm, David's perspective changes, and this all-seeing God has become his greatest comfort. You'll learn why by the end of this chapter.

Our popular American culture has watered down this true and living God with cheap slogans and shallow clichés. I've seen bumper stickers with a smiley face that say, "Smile! God Loves You" and t-shirts that say, "God Loves You" and even "Jesus Is My Homeboy." Such cavalier views of God often indicate that the driver or wearer doesn't know the true and living God, the God David knew. Throughout the Bible, when God shows up in various forms or visions, people are absolutely terrified. Some even fall to their face as though dead. This response is natural and even reflexive because God is incomprehensibly awesome in every sense of the word. We are foolish to assume—as popular culture dangerously does—that if God exists, He is only a loving and caring God. Plenty of instances throughout history and maybe even in our own life seem to show the opposite. Ideals are peaceful; history is violent.

BOSS GOD VS. FATHER GOD

Let's back up a bit. We've already seen that for us to have a real, objective hope—to have EPIC Hope—God must exist, and He must speak. Furthermore, this God must be knowable, transcendent, and immanent—and incredibly, the Bible says that God is all that. But what if this entire creating-and-running-the-world thing is strictly business for God? What if He is like a micromanaging boss at a Fortune 500 company? In the world of corporate America, you're more of a cog in the grand machine than you are an individual person with feelings and desires. You are a means to an end (profit), and you are replaceable if you don't perform. Such a boss may give you a second, even a third chance if you mess up, but not because he or she cares about you, but because it's more of a hassle to hire and train someone new—and you do the job well enough.

While living with John and Stacey, I thought a lot and wrote a lot about "Boss God." I realized I'd been seeing God as a boss—and torturing myself. You see, because of my past wreckage and struggles with sin, I felt like a failed employee in God's company. By that time, three bosses at three companies had fired me, and one of the jobs had been with a Fortune 500 company. I always seemed to disappoint people. *If this was how imperfect, sinful people viewed me, how much more clearly is God seeing my flaws and sins?* Projecting this negative thought onto God, I lived feeling as if I were always on the verge of getting fired by God.

Before the wheels of my life fell off, I never struggled with how God viewed me or with feeling loved by God. I took for granted this Christian truth because the wheels of life were spinning smoothly. I was an up-and-coming Christian star, devoted to serving God, bringing people into His kingdom, bringing Him glory, and bringing in heavenly profits. I was a useful employee. Why wouldn't God love me?

Also, I had never understood why people with absent or abusive fathers struggled to see God as a loving Father. My dad was always present and loving, so viewing God this way was no real stretch for me. But then the wheels started to jam, they stalled, and then they just fell off. I had my struggles, and my ex-wife had hers. Her struggle was controlling a razor-sharp tongue that knew my most vulnerable spots—and those words didn't stop until I fled the house. This person I loved so much seemed to hate me and was quite adept at letting me know—often. I would run and hide in a motel and drink till I fell asleep. This, of course, compounded my problems: I got fired from multiple jobs, which fueled the fires at home.

Hardly surprising, this is when Boss God first emerged in my life. I had become a poor employee who was losing the company lots of money. Boss God just stood there, arms crossed and silent, having on His face that look of frustration and disappointment—termination papers in hand. God took on the image of a harsh taskmaster much like the Pharaohs of old. God tolerated me because of Jesus, but He didn't like me, let alone love me. How could He? I knew myself better than anyone except God did—and *I* didn't even like me.

Now, I can imagine a fellow Christian reading this and thinking, *Didn't you understand the gospel? Didn't you understand grace?* Yes! Absolutely! I had a sound theology, a firm grasp of the gospel, and a coherent and godly worldview. But my misperceptions about God and myself indicate that life is messier than we Christians like to admit. Expert knowledge and sound theology do not automate sinless living and healthy emotions. Remember my old pastor's warning to me? "Be careful, my boy. Your knowledge is way beyond your sanctification."

Yes, a sound theology undergirding biblical belief in a knowable, transcendent, immanent God is a necessary condition for real objective hope, but it's not sufficient. Belief in **theism** alone leaves us with Boss God. And since hope and love often live together and die together, we need more than a philosophically cool Boss God.

A PARENT'S HEART

I struggled with Boss God for several years. Honestly, I still struggle at times. After I married Rebekah, I used to drive my son to his elementary school in the mornings. I didn't have to; I just wanted to spend time with him. We always arrived early to work a little on his homework. One morning, while helping him with math, I had an epiphany.

My son was wrestling with math... and not winning. I saw that he wanted to do it right and that he was genuinely trying, but he couldn't get it. I knew he wanted to please me by showing me he could do it: *I'm smart, too, Daddy. Just like the other kids.* I saw and felt the discouragement in his little heart. I saw him wanting to throw it all away and give up. I saw his heart, and it broke my heart. That's when the epiphany came: *What if God views me like that? What if God is not a Boss God, but instead, like me, is a loving Parent grieving for the hurt in His kid's heart?*

Sitting there with my boy, I saw his *effort* and his *desire* to please me, and that's what mattered. His heart mattered, not some stupid letter grade on a piece of paper. Then I thought about the many parents who act like Boss God. I thought about those parents who only care about straight As and top scores. I thought about those parents who don't tolerate Bs or even A minuses. They care more about how they look to the world or about their child's future "success" than they care about the heart of their child. That, too, made me sad because I know how the Boss God's presence in my life had tortured me.

Seeing my son try yet fail, I loved him all the more! I wanted to take all his homework and do it for him. I wanted to see him succeed and feel confident. His desire and effort were what I saw, and that state of his heart mattered to me far more than any outcome. His pain became my pain, but I believe mine outweighed his.

What if God is like that—like a caring parent—but even more so? If I—an imperfect and selfish, sinful human—deeply love my kids even when they struggle and fail, and if my heart breaks for them, how much more our perfectly loving Father must feel compassion for us, His kids? How much more must He love us when we fail? In fact, what if God—this true and living God I talk about—loves His children unconditionally? What if God knows everything about me, past, present, and future, and still loves me completely? And if that is true—and I believe with every ounce of my being that it is—what if we really believed it?

NO DECODER JESUS NEEDED

As I recognized the incorrect and thus harmful ways I was seeing God, I realized that I associated Boss God with God the Father. I felt like Jesus could understand me better and therefore could sympathize with me more in my struggles. Same with God the Holy Spirit. I realized that my existential pain-points of fear and shame were in relation to the way I was thinking about God the Father.[42]

As I said, I viewed the Father standing in front of me, arms folded, gripping my termination papers so tightly His knuckles were white. He didn't like me, but He tolerated me only because of Jesus. Let me explain.

Remember when you were a kid and you got a pair of those decoder glasses that allowed you to see a secret message or an

---

42 The Bible teaches that God is Trinitarian in nature, meaning the one God exists in three Persons: the Father, the Son, and the Holy Spirit. Each of these eternal Persons is distinct yet They are all of the same essence. Each Person is fully God and possesses all the attributes of the one true God. The Bible also reveals that each Person of the Godhead appears to have unique roles or tasks in relation to creation and redemption. It's a deep topic, and it's a central doctrine of Christian theology that is well established in the Bible.

image inside another random image or series of scribbles? Maybe you ordered a pair from a magazine; maybe you got a pair in a cereal box. Well, I realized I was thinking of Jesus as a pair of decoder glasses that God the Father used when He looked at me. To be more specific, I believed that when God the Father looked at me *through* Jesus, He saw me as He saw Jesus: holy, pure, and sinless. But if Jesus stepped aside and the Father saw me for who I really am, He'd smite me in a second. And because I thought about the Father that way, it felt[43] like He only loved me because of Jesus. And we—the Father and I—both knew the truth: if Jesus quit being my bodyguard, I'd be dead meat.[44]

Where did I get this idea? I'm not sure, but maybe we Christians tend to focus on Jesus' great love but hear—relatively speaking—little about the Father's love for us. When I turned to God's Word concerning this issue, I found great comfort. The Bible sets forth the truth that God the Father has loved us from all eternity, which means long before Jesus and the cross. *No, God the Father doesn't love me because of Jesus. The Father loves me because... He just does!* Consider the most famous verse in the Bible: *God [the Father] so loved the world that He [the Father] gave His one and only Son, that whoever believes in Him [Jesus] shall not perish*

---

43 When I write, I'm very deliberate about the words I use to refer to feeling, thinking, believing, and knowing. Christians tend to focus on thinking and truth while ignoring, denying or, worse, vilifying feelings. But our feelings are an integral part of our humanity and part of the image of God in us even though they get us in trouble at times. But bad or poor thinking also gets us into trouble. My brokenness during those days gave rise to a host of chaotic emotions that led to my having wrong views about God and about myself. This was definitely a feelings-dominated chapter in my life. Getting back to the truth enabled me to start putting back together the pieces of my life.

44 In an article titled "How Do You Think of Your Heavenly Father?" Erik Raymond wrote this: "The second concern that I have is our perception of our heavenly Father in merely legal terms. Because we love the doctrine of justification, those in the Reformed camp are particularly susceptible to this temptation. Justification is the legal declaration of the sinner, by God the Father, as righteous based upon the doing and dying of Jesus and in spite of our persistent and pervasive depravity. How can you ever get over this? We can't! It consumes so much of what we think about. We are walking around knowing that we sin and [that we] are sinners, but God declares us righteous because of Christ! C'mon! But we can, if we are not careful, eclipse God's Fatherly goodness by only focusing on him as judge. God is not less than a judge, but he is much, much more." (https://www.thegospelcoalition.org/blogs/erik-raymond/how-do-you-think-of-your-heavenly-father/)

but have eternal life (John 3:16 NIV). And it was God the Father who sacrificed His beloved Son to make a way of redemption for you and me so we could get back home to Him. The Father's love not only preceded Jesus' mission to earth; God's love planned it.

Want more proof? How about from Jesus Himself? On the evening of His arrest, Jesus prayed to His Father what we often call the High Priestly Prayer. The role of Jewish priests was to go before God on behalf of the people to, for instance, offer sacrifices and plead for forgiveness. In this prayer Jesus was acting as a priest and mediator on behalf of His people—present and future—who would believe and follow Him. Jesus prayed to God that His followers would be unified as one so that *"the world will know that You [Father God] sent Me and have loved them even as You [Father God] have loved Me"* (John 17:23). Did you see that? God the Father loves us as much as He loved Jesus. Wrap your head around that![45]

BECAUSE HE LOVES YOU. PERIOD.

God didn't *have* to send Jesus into this world, nor did Jesus *have* to die and atone for sin. Nothing forced God to make a way of redemption. He could have folded up the whole dang thing and started over. Nothing forced Jesus to walk this earth; He came here because He wanted to. God wanted something, and what He wanted carried an almost unbelievable price tag. God wanted something that would require an eternity-shaking sacrifice. But in God's estimation, the cost was worth it.

What did God want so much?

Us.

I don't know if you're like me, but that truth makes me feel

---

45 See also Deuteronomy 7:6-8; Psalm 68:5-6; 103:13-14; Matthew 18:14; Colossians 1:12-13; Romans 8:15, 28-39; Ephesians 1:3-5 and 2:4; and 1 John 4:10.

quite uncomfortable. Apparently I'm not alone. Erik Raymond says most of us react with a "theological flinch."[46] We flinch at the bare truth of God's love and rush to add theological qualifiers. We say things like "Yes, God loves us because Jesus removed our sins," or we slip in God's attributes of grace and mercy or the truth of election. We say things like "Yes, God loves us in Christ so that we can carry out the Great Commission and bring Him glory."[47] And we do that because the idea that God simply loves me apart from what I can do for Him or will do for Him—and that God loves me apart from Jesus' work on the cross—seems too good to be true. When we understand the holy nature of God and our own objective sin and guilt, it just feels wrong to sit with the bare truth that God loves me as me. Period.

And this isn't only a New Testament idea. This is who God *is*. Consider these verses from the Old Testament that highlight this liberating truth. Moses was talking to the nation of Israel:

> The LORD *your God has chosen you to be a people for Himself, a special treasure above all the peoples on the face of the earth. The* LORD *did not set His love on you nor choose you because you were more in number than any other people, for you were the least of all peoples;* but because the LORD loves you, *and because He would keep the oath which He swore to your fathers.* (Deuteronomy 7:6-8)

Did you notice? No qualifiers there! God chose you simply because He loves you. Sit with that for a while.

---

46 Erik Raymond, *Basking in God's Love* (https://www.placefortruth.org/blog/basking-in-gods-love)
47 All these statements are true. I agree with Jonathan Edwards's essay "The End for Which God Created the World" and, in our time, John Piper's *God's Passion for His Own Glory*: God's main purpose in all creation is not human happiness but, rather, to magnify His own awesome Self. Piper added you and me to that picture by pointing out that "God is most glorified in us when we are most satisfied in Him." My point in this section is not to elevate us or our happiness above God's glory, but to show the oft overlooked fact that God loves us and wants to be in relationship with us, not because we can or will do things for Him, but just because He does. He wants us because He loves us.

God loves you and wants you to be in relationship with Him.

THE GREATEST CHAPTER EVER

Jesus died. Never forget that.

Jesus died. His body was a corpse. His followers wrapped His body in cloth and spices to mask the scent of death.

Jesus died. A couple of His followers, brokenhearted and confused, placed His body in a stone tomb.

Three days passed.

God raised Him from the dead (Acts 13:30).

This is a record of history.

Victory.

TO WHAT LENGTHS!

What I want you to see in this chapter is to what lengths God went to bring us home, to be in relationship with us. Twenty years after first learning about this, I still shake my head. Who *is* this God? Who would do something so... so audaciously, unselfishly, astoundingly heroic? And for what? For me? Yes, me! And you! And I know all this, yet too often I still treat God like dirt....

I stop typing. I move my hands from the keyboard... I sit back, arms crossed, face serious... puzzled. I ponder.... Then I bow. *My God. My King. My Savior. My Father.*

The cross of Christ is the greatest proof of God's passionate love for us. The cross gives us a glimpse of how much we are worth to God. Sadly, throughout history, the church has tended to focus on how unworthy we sinners are, and our sin is a truth we absolutely cannot ignore. You and I are unworthy of—and unable to earn—God's love and acceptance. But that is not the same as saying we are without worth, that we are worthless. Our worth is, in fact, incalculable. And God demonstrates our worth *to* Him in the extreme lengths He went to bring us to Himself. Paul put it like this:

> Who, being in very nature God, did not consider equality with God something to be used to his own advantage; rather, he made himself nothing by taking the very nature of a servant, being made in human likeness. And being found in appearance as a man, he humbled himself by becoming obedient to death—even death on a cross! (Philippians 2:6-8 NIV)

THREE EYE-OPENERS TO HELP YOU SEE HOPE

When I think about *this* God and *this* love in *this* way, I experience its power to bring profound freedom and hope, to bring EPIC Hope. When I think about *this* God and *this* love in *this* way, I find freedom from the Boss God who incites fear, shame, perfectionism, and hopelessness. And every believer needs that freedom. Finally, this focus on God's love for me opens my eyes to EPIC Hope in at least three ways.

First, I realize that when I struggle with knowing God's love for me, it's because I'm thinking about God from a Unitarian or deistic perspective instead of from the biblical Trinitarian view. Unitarianism, like deism, sees God as one being and one person, not as the tri-unity of Persons that the Bible teaches. When I see God as Boss God, the harsh Taskmaster who merely tolerates me, it's because I've forgotten the gospel, the wonderfully good news of Jesus. I've forgotten about the miracle of His incarnation: the transcendent Word became immanent flesh. I've forgotten about His suffering on the cross. I've forgotten about what seemingly insane lengths this Triune God went to in order to redeem me.

When we lose sight of the cross, we naturally start to see God as strictly the Judge of Heaven, the demanding Taskmaster who cares only about our grades—our performance—and not about our hearts or who we are as individuals. Understanding and embracing God's love for us will help us destroy Boss God—a false god—and return to our loving Father, *the God of hope* (Romans 15:13).

Second, when I keep the cross in view, I realize that God doesn't merely tolerate me; God loves me more than I will ever know this side of heaven, and He went to extreme lengths to be in relationship with me. God wants to be in relationship with me. Think about it this way. Jesus didn't come into this world, take on human flesh, suffer betrayal, undergo excruciating physical torture, let Himself be the focus of the full wrath of God, and then die only to have none of that count for anything because of our sin and lack of obedience. Furthermore, what would it mean if, after all that, God kept us at arm's length, barely tolerating us because we're still sinners? It would mean that God did not consider Jesus' life, death, and resurrection enough to cover our sin. But the cross—God's eternal plan for our salvation—absolutely covers our sin. At the cross, Jesus *obtained eternal redemption* and paid for all our sins *once for all* (Hebrews 9:12).

Still, when it comes to our resting in God's love, we may still too often be the girl pulling petals from a daisy: "He loves me. He loves me not." When we're good, He loves me! But when we're bad, He loves me not. That plucked-daisy god is a god made in our own image; that god is not the true and living God. As Dutch-American theologian Geerhardus Vos (1862-1949) put it, "The best proof that [God] will never cease to love us lies in that He never began." Knowing that God loves us simply for His own good pleasure—and that He will love us always and forever—further helps to eradicate Boss God and get out of our existential prisons of shame, guilt, and fear.

Third, I realize that God loves me *more* than He loves the quality of my performance—good or bad. This is the epiphany I got while helping my son with his math homework. We need to understand that God knew exactly what He was getting when He saved us. Nothing will ever surprise God, so He can't ever be disappointed. From eternity, God has known every sin I will ever commit, yet He loves me. He knew what He was getting when He redeemed us. People around us may view us like a beaten-up, broken-down jalopy—but not God. Instead, as Paul wrote, *we are His workmanship*, His *masterpiece*, His poem (see Ephesians 2:10). Besides, God loves restoration projects.

So, is God concerned about our performance and our actions? Absolutely. But most of us already know that all too well. In fact, most of us focus solely on our performance, and we make the Christian life only about *not* sinning. As Dallas Willard said, our focus shifts toward "sin management."[48] We need to stop thinking that we need to get straight A's before God will crack a smile. That's Boss God, and we are trying to get away from him. We need to realize—and this is the wonderful, liberating truth of the gospel—that Jesus took all our classes, earned all A-pluses, and put those on our report card. Jesus gave the Father His perfect record but wrote our name at the top. And remember, it was the Father who planned this entire project to begin with! May we realize how free we can be—if we let ourselves—from the tyranny of perfection.

That is grace. As Paul wrote, *By grace you have been saved through faith, and that not of yourselves; it is the gift of God* (Ephesians 2:8). The Christian life is one of freedom from the

---

48 Dallas Willard, *The Divine Conspiracy* (Harper Collins, 1998) chapter 2.

law of perfection (Jesus fulfilled that law for us) and confident assurance that God's grace is sufficient to cover our sin. For the Christian, it's okay to not be okay. It's okay to be weak. It's okay to fail. It's okay to be human because God *knows how we are formed; He remembers that we are dust* (see Psalm 103:11-14). In addition, when we are weak, we can know God as our strength (see 2 Corinthians 12:9).

Now consider more of Timothy Keller's wisdom: "If you are not fully convinced of God's love for you, suffering will tear you apart."[49] Yet knowing about God's love in our head is not the same as being fully convinced of God's love in our heart. I still struggle with this. I fight Boss God often and must remind myself of the very truths I laid out in this chapter. But I also admit that understanding and believing these truths has brought me to a new level of personal freedom and existential peace.

Finally, if we aren't solidly grounded in God's true, unconditional, and eternal love, EPIC Hope is not possible. Without God's genuine, unconditional, eternal love, hope dies… and when hope dies, we die. Love is a necessary condition of EPIC Hope, but one last condition must be met if we are to live with EPIC Hope. We turn to that condition now.

---

49 Keller, 52.

CHAPTER 17

EPIC HOPE #5: THERE IS LIFE AFTER DEATH

I THINK ABOUT DEATH a lot. You do too. We all do. We can't help it because it's the single most inescapable, horrific fact of our existence. We are all going to die—and probably sooner than we'd like.

I know, I know, a splendid way to end a book on hope! But it's the most glaring reality and the most widely proven fact... that we refuse to acknowledge. Why? Obviously, death terrifies us. The Bible says that before any of us know the true and living God, our fear of death keeps us bound like slaves (Hebrews 2:15).

The fact of our death is a constant and frightening threat that can hold us captive. Both this fear and the sense of being in captivity become more severe the older we get, as we check off yet another decade. Just yesterday, I was seventeen years old and roaming the halls of my high school, looking cool, and thinking about girls. Snap my fingers, and I'm 42 and roaming the halls of Costco, looking at multivitamins, and thinking about getting my twenty-year-old daughter through her last year of college. Tomorrow, God willing, I'll be roaming the halls of AARP, looking for discounts from Costco on Centrum Silver, and thinking about the long trek back to wherever I parked my dang car.

Snap! Snap! Snap! Snap! Done.

———

It baffles me that people go through life and never contemplate the **big questions** like *Where did we and everything come from? Why is there something instead of nothing? Does God exist? If so, who is God, and can we know this Being? Is the Bible really what it claims to be? What and who am I? What happens after I die?* You know, questions like those. But then again, I get it. I understand because before God opened my eyes, I never wasted my time on such trivial matters either. I had way more important things to figure out, like finding enough money for a Taco Bell run and trying to get Jill (my high school girlfriend) back after she dumped me (she didn't take me back; she was smart).

Since getting saved, though, I am happily plagued by such questions. In the early days of my Christian life, when I was pondering eternity and human history, the idea that our life is a blip on the screen captivated me. The Bible says our lives here are a shadow, a vapor, and a blink. And I saw this in black and white....

About 15 years ago, evangelist Ray Comfort hired me to do the illustrations for his *Evidence Bible.* He gave me 20 words, and I had to create a graphic to illustrate each one. For the word *mortality*, I created a numeric chart that showed approximately how many hours a person has left to live. Using the average endpoint age of 70, I showed about how many hours you have left to live if you are 20 years old, or 30, or 40, and so on. It's alarming. Mortality is alarming.

As I said, I thought a lot about these issues back in my twenties.

I thought about the billions of people who existed in history, who had loves and desires and hopes just like mine, but who are now long gone and—the vast majority—forgotten. Totally forgotten.

Now, let me clarify: I do not have some morbid fascination with death and dying. This kind of pondering is more about my faith than about death. Christianity allows me... No, Christianity *frees* me from being enslaved by death's threat; my faith helps me move from denial toward reality.

But I get it, friend. This is way freaky stuff! To think that you only have so many hours left to live—and when you see it in numbers, it's always way less than you think—is enough to bring on some serious anxiety and depression. It's not that I don't feel that, too; it's just that I'm largely free from its tyranny.

The EPIC Hope that Rebekah and I share gives us the courage to face the fact that we will die. So in this last chapter, I want to share with you the most exciting benefit we have right now because we are followers of Jesus. This benefit has astounded me, thrilled me, transformed me, and freed me more than anything else God has promised us believers. I could talk about other benefits like heaven, new resurrected bodies, or no more sin and pain. I could talk about a new earth, streets of gold, or heavenly dwellings. But here I want to focus on one idea. It's something that Jesus talked a lot about and something that makes all those other future benefits possible. It's the idea that I have eternal life right now.

THE LAST CONDITION FOR EPIC HOPE

Hope in all its forms is a future-oriented desire and a future-oriented matter. As Paul said, we don't hope for what we have or for what we see right now (Romans 8:24-25). And that future-oriented hope always involves our well-being or the well-being of someone we care about. We all want assurance that we'll make it.

But there's one future fact that sometimes whispers and sometimes shouts, "You may win minor victories here or there, but soon enough, you'll take your last breath." This statement is more than a threat. It's a certainty. It's death.

The last condition necessary for real, objective, EPIC Hope is... immortality. Whether or not we are aware or are able to acknowledge this fact, immortality is our single greatest human desire and hope. I think—whether conscious or unconscious—the fear of death motivates much of our behavior. It motivates us to eat better, go to the gym, search for a mate, work hard to make money, acquire bigger and better things, go to church, save for retirement, create a legacy, and do good works. Yet the terror of death can lead us to fear, anxiety, depression, and despair, and these often lead us to forms of escapism (for instance, alcohol, drugs, hedonism, workaholism, suicide). No matter what we try or what we do, we can't escape the dreadful promise of our death. We experiment with many creative cloaks in an attempt to cover the hourglass and forget about the sand running through it. But we know the hourglass is always there, reminding us that we are ever closer to the last chapter of our story. Without immortality, we have no hope for beyond the grave.

Philosopher William Lane Craig offered this perspective:

> With no hope of immortality, man's life leads only to the grave. His life is but a spark in the infinite blackness, a spark that appears, flickers, and dies forever. Compared to the infinite stretch of time, the span of man's life is but an infinitesimal moment; and yet this is all the life he will ever know. Therefore, everyone must come face to face with what theologian Paul Tillich has called "the threat of non-being." For though I know now that I exist, that I am alive, I also know that someday I will no longer exist, that I will

no longer be, that I will die. This thought is staggering and threatening: to think that the person I call "myself" will cease to exist, that I will be no more!... As the French existentialist Jean-Paul Sartre observed, "Several hours or several years make no difference once you have lost eternity."[50]

I've met many people who say that they don't fear death. Maybe so, but it's probably because they haven't thought specifically about their own death. Craig continues:

Sartre observed that death is not threatening so long as we view it as the death of the other, from a third-person standpoint, so to speak. It is only when we internalize it and look at it from the first-person perspective—"my death: I am going to die"—that the threat of non-being becomes real... One can even look at one's own death from the third-person standpoint, as if it were the death of another or even of an animal... but the true existential significance of my death can only be appreciated from the first-person perspective, as I realize that I am going to die and forever cease to exist. My life is just a momentary transition out of oblivion into oblivion.[51]

Like I said, way freaky stuff. Crushing, actually.

IT'S JUST WRONG!

I said earlier in this chapter that our death is the most glaring reality and the most widely proven fact that we refuse to acknowledge. And we refuse because death terrifies us. But there's another reason for this refusal: death and dying feel very, very wrong.

Now from an atheistic and evolutionary perspective, what is, just is, and you're back in that whole accidental spark on the timeline

---

50 William Lane Craig, *Reasonable Faith* (Crossway Books, 1984), p. 57.
51 Ibid., p. 58.

thing and life being nothing more than a "momentary transition out of oblivion into oblivion." Death's not wrong; death just *is*.[52] In the end, you are not fundamentally different from a dog, a mollusk, or a dirt clod. Everything—and that includes us—just disintegrates back into the elements. The process is completely natural.

But even those who profess to believe that becoming worm food is our destiny don't live that way. I don't care what your professed belief is, the fact of death *feels* horribly wrong. We feel like we should live forever. Furthermore, death brings nothing but brokenness to this world. It's 100 percent destructive. And from a Christian perspective, our intense feelings about death confirm what we all know: death and dying *are* wrong. Death and dying were not part of God's original design for mankind. Death emerged as a result of sin. To **Adam and Eve**, God said, *"By the sweat of your brow you will eat your food until you return to the ground, since from it you were taken; for dust you are and to dust you will return"* (Genesis 3:18; see also Romans 5:12).

We are far more than animated biological bags of stuff; we also possess an invisible life force referred to as our soul, spirit, or mind. Whatever you want to call it, you are far more than your body. In addition, we are all uniquely made in the image of God, and He has placed a longing for eternity in our hearts (Ecclesiastes3:11). God made us the crown of His creation. Of course He didn't design us to die and cease existing—and *we know this*.

THE BEST NEWS EVER!

Before becoming a Christian, I never thought much about death or life after death for two reasons. First, I didn't think much

---

52 From an atheistic and evolutionary perspective, there is no universal basis for objective "right" or "wrong." To have an objective morality—to have right and wrong, good and evil—you need certain metaphysical conditions, such as a fixed, universal, separate standard that is enforced independently of humans. Those are some necessary conditions to begin with to establish an objective ethic. The God of the Bible alone fulfills those requirements.

about meaningful issues. I was cool but not too bright. Second, I did what we all do: I made cloaks of distraction to cover the hourglass. But when I met Jesus—the *real* Jesus—He looked back at me; He looked deep into my empty soul. I had not stumbled upon a trendy philosophy or a new idea. I had encountered a Person—the true and living God to whom I have to one day give an account of my life. And in that moment I saw and I felt my emptiness, my brokenness, and my guilt. And as never before, I felt how fragile my life was; I faced my mortality. Jesus pulled all the cloaks off my hourglass. Everything else in my life seemed to fade away as my eternal destiny came into focus. I knew that if I died at that moment, I would go to hell—whatever that was.

When people in the Bible encountered Jesus and His angelic representatives, this kind of awakening was common. People would ask Jesus, *"What must I do to inherit eternal life?"* and *"What must I do to be saved?"* Whenever people encounter the real Jesus today, one of two things happens: they awaken to the fact of their mortality, or they feel threatened and harden their hearts. When people sincerely had questions, Jesus responded with tenderness and compassion. He saw people as scattered and lost sheep without a Shepherd.

Jesus talked about a lot of important issues, but one central teaching He often hit upon was that of eternal life—and He offered eternal life to anyone who wanted it.[53] The Bible says this:

> *God so loved the world that He gave His only begotten Son, that whoever believes in Him should not perish but **have***

---

53 If Jesus were not God incarnate, this offer of eternal life would be ludicrous. It would also be clear evidence that Jesus was a liar or a lunatic, as C. S. Lewis so famously put it. Jesus doesn't allow people to be neutral about Him. Jesus Himself said, *"He who is not with me is against Me"* (Matthew 12:30). Jesus also said, *"Do you suppose that I came to give [phony, shallow] peace on earth? I tell you, not at all, but rather division"* (Luke 12:51). Because Jesus often claimed to be God, the Jewish leaders—threatened by this—often tried to kill Jesus, and they ultimately manipulated the Romans into doing it for them.

everlasting life.... For God did not send His Son into the world to condemn the world, but that the world through Him might be **saved**. (John 3:16-17; see also 5:24; 6:47; 10:28; et al.)

Now, I don't have a single come-to-faith moment I can point to; I can't tell you about a time when the heavens opened and I got saved. I'm not even sure if I was eighteen or nineteen when it happened. (Remember, my eighteen-year-old brain was working at low capacity!) But I clearly remember—and will never forget—what it meant to me to *know that I was saved*. It was quite literally, life-changing. My eyes opened, and for the first time I saw the world as God's beautiful creation. I noticed colors, trees, clouds, and other people as God's handiwork. God forgave my sin. All of it. Forever. My life had meaning and purpose beyond trying to make money, find girls, party, and look cool. I realized I was part of something big, something cosmic, something Epic. But what I remember most—what hit me the hardest and overwhelmed me with a sense of freedom—was that I had eternal life. And I still have eternal life, and I will never *not* have it. I will never die!

HOPE THAT CHANGES EVERYTHING

If you haven't yet experienced this kind of moment—this kind of life-changing realization—for yourself, know that it's hard for me to put into words the depth of joy and freedom that you feel when you really grasp the fact that you will never die. I still feel this joy and freedom today, twenty-something years later. Very few ideas in this life carry such enduring power.

As a new Christian—I was twenty—I was so rocked by this newfound truth, that I quit my job as a graphic designer and got hired at a little Chevron gas station during the graveyard shift. For four years I showed up there with my Bible, a stack of books, and my laptop. The job basically required just a warm body through the night, and that's exactly the kind of job I wanted. I wanted a job that would pay me to study God's Word!

My shift started at 10:00 p.m., and I drove out there around 8:00 to pray to this God, my God. I had found a hill that overlooked the busy 5 freeway. I always grabbed a lawn chair out of the back of my little Ford Ranger, set it up on the hilltop, sat in the dark, and just talked to God. I prayed with my eyes open, looking down at the thousands of bustling cars. Joy and gratitude flooded me every time because I was free from that fake rat race of life. All the pressure and anxiety I'd felt as a young man trying to figure out life, trying to check off all the boxes and climb the ladder of success, trying to find my spot in the rat race—all of that was gone. As I sat up there on that hill and watched all those people on the freeway coming to and from work, I felt like God had plucked me out of that frantic stream of chaos and set me on top of that hill. What caused me to feel free from it all? Eternal life. I would live forever. God smashed my hourglass and replaced it with Himself. I had *the hope of eternal life* (Titus 1:2; 3:7).

And today, knowing that I have eternal life allows me to let go of my life. You see, Jesus taught this seemingly odd principle that *"He who finds his life will lose it, and he who loses his life for my sake will find it"* (Matthew 10:39). In other words, if you try to take control of your life and be your own god, you'll lose your life not just after you die, but right here and now. You'll become filled with anxiety and exhausted by your efforts to manipulate situations and relationships for your own ends. The tighter you grip your life, the more you lose it. But if you give your life back to the One who owns it anyway, He will give you new life, and you will find your purpose.

I no longer need to manipulate things or people to fit with my agenda because the One who rules over time and eternity uncovered my hourglass and shattered it. So I don't have to freak out because time is running out and I'm not yet at a certain (fake) stage in life. And I don't have to freak out because God has lifted my life out of time and into eternity.

In chapter 14 we talked about God's Grand Narrative, and I said that our life here and now is not a dress rehearsal for heaven. Life here and now is significant and purposeful. What I'm saying in this chapter does not conflict with that truth. That we are in God's Grand Narrative tells us that this life is real, significant, and purposeful. That we have eternal life, however, helps us not take ourselves and our plans too seriously. We can chill out a bit because, ultimately, my life is God's Story, not mine. But the really cool thing is, God invites me to be a co-producer of His Story. My life and my decisions are therefore important, but I don't have the final word, nor is it all up to me to pull off the plan. The show will never end for me, and that truth frees me to let go, sit back, and enjoy the journey. I am free to Live NOW!

MORE THAN MERELY AN EXTENSION

I want to point out one more feature about eternal life: It's a mistake to think that eternal life is something afforded to me only after my body dies. The truth is, I have eternal life *right now*. I have already passed from death into life.

The eternal life that God offers is both quantitative and qualitative. Most of us think, *Eternal life? Cool! I'll live forever.* But living is far more than marking time. To begin with, our problems with hope and hopelessness find no solution if we're merely passing time on the planet.

Without God, the mere extension of life into eternity would simply mean an endless existence. Without God, life has no ultimate meaning, purpose, value, or hope. Thus if we had eternal life but no God, we would have to endure an endless life that had no real meaning, purpose, value, or hope. Eternal life *without* God would be prison, not freedom.

Many other popular ideas about life after death are thrown around. But upon examination, every one of them ends up either annihilating life, reducing it to absurdity, or making it sheer torment.

- *Annihilating life:* Most pantheistic systems like Buddhism and New Age teach that when we die, our soul or life force is absorbed or reabsorbed back into the one ultimate life force. You and everything that makes you—*you,* disappears and is absorbed into the One. Yeah, real exciting.

- *Reducing life to absurdity*: We need only look to the various ideas of reincarnation. To think that some impersonal force is watching every life form, keeping score, tallying up the points, and then reassigning everyone and everything to a new form—so that you can come back as a different person, a dog, a toad, or a peanut—is just absurd.

- *Making life sheer torment:* Many people believe that when we die, our disembodied spirits get trapped either here or between dimensions and consigned as ghosts that roam the earth, inhabit houses, or hang out in graveyards. As ghosts, they're trying to resolve past conflicts and/or make peace with those "on the other side." Or maybe they only want to spook people by opening cupboards, moving chairs, and moaning creepily in the night. Yep, that's both realistic and something to look forward to—not! If I were a creepy ghost in someone's attic, I'd freak myself out. I would call Ghostbusters because there's some creepy-ass ghost up here. *Oh, that's me. Crap!*

These views of "life" after death are not only devoid of empowering hope, but they would be a form of endless torment.

Therefore, merely an extension of time does not contribute to real, empowering hope. We human beings need both immortality *and* God, the true God. The Bible teaches that when your body dies, *you*—yes, *you*—continue on either with God in glory, in what we call heaven, or without God in hell. But *you* stay *you*. Furthermore, when God wraps up this whole Grand Narrative and you have committed your life to Jesus, God will resurrect your original body—the DNA, molecules, atoms—recreate it in a glorified form, and reunite it with your soul. If God can speak everything into existence, then resurrecting and recreating the original building blocks of your body is cake.

The Bible also says that God is going to make a new earth that we will inhabit and where we will create a whole new civilization with God reigning as King. The Bible doesn't give too many details about all this, but the few it gives sound awesome. People who, on earth, made the commitment to believe and follow Jesus will have a special place in heaven God made just for them. We will meet up with many of our friends and loved ones. Whatever heaven is and however it will look, it will be—as the Bible says—glorious.

Now, as for eternal life in the here and now, I can tell you that eternal life colors and baptizes every aspect of my life 24/7. God wants me—and you—to live life to the fullest (John 10:10). I lived as a non-Christian for about 20 years, and I've lived as a Christian for about 22 years. There's no stinkin' comparison! The Christian life, while sometimes difficult and confusing, is nonetheless uniquely a life of profound joy, peace, love, satisfaction, wisdom, and hope. I'm never alone in this big, crazy world. I get to play a special part in God's EPIC Grand Story. I'm loved like crazy by the God of creation. God forgives all my sins and wrongs. I live in peace and love with my spouse, my kids, my family, my friends, and even strangers. I'm content with where I am in life because I'm right where God wants me. I'm saved and can do nothing to undo that. I have eternal life right now, and I will never die. All these amazing truths make life not just worth living, but downright exciting. These truths also free me to really Live NOW, and whenever I do die, it will be far better (Philippians 1:21-23; Romans 8:18, 30).

DEATH IS SWALLOWED UP

I've seen only one dead body in my life, up close and personal: my dad.

Cancer took my dad about four years ago. For two weeks, Rebekah, my sister, my bro-in-law, and I took shifts so that someone was with him around the clock. A couple days before he died, he slipped into a coma. Three weeks before that, however, he had called me and asked me to come over to explain to him how he could get right with God and know for sure that he would go to heaven. I had told him years before that I didn't want to be in heaven without him. He never forgot those words. So I explained to my dad the marvelous news of the gospel, we held hands, and both of us prayed.

After he went into his coma, we sat around his bed, holding his hands, and telling him it was okay for him to go. We realized that even though he was in a coma, he could still hear us or sense us, and every time we talked, he fought to stay here. So we all stayed quiet until he took his last breath. It was a heavy and unnerving experience. My dad was dead. Dads and moms aren't supposed to die. But they do. Kids aren't supposed to die. But they do. My dad was dead.

Some minutes later, I went back into his room. It was only the two of us. I sat next to him and took his hand. It was lifeless. I talked to him. I told him what a good dad he had been. I caressed his face, that face that always smiled at me and loved me and supported me. I kissed him on the forehead and said, "I love you, Daddy." My dad was dead. But there were certain things that I knew—and I knew he wasn't actually dead.

Remember from chapter 15, when I said that Jesus died and His body was a corpse? Jesus' body was dead like my dad's body. But Jesus, like my dad, was not dead. (The Bible reveals that when we are absent from the body (i.e. dead) we are alive in the presence of God (see 2 Corinthians 5:8). When our eyes close here for the last time, they immediately open there.) God resurrected Jesus' dead body and brought it back to life, but in a new, and glorified state. As Paul said, Jesus was *changed* and *transformed* (1 Corinthians 15). Jesus' resurrection was God's global declaration that He had defeated death. Our greatest human enemy—death—was put to death by Christ's resurrection: *Death has been swallowed up in victory* is what Paul said about the resurrection of Christ as well as believers:

> *Where, O death is your victory?*
> *Where, O death, is your sting? (1 Corinthians 15:54)*

Jesus was the Forerunner of all who die in faith. Because He rose and lives again, we who believe will also rise and live again as well (1 Corinthians 15:52-53).

THOSE WHO HAVE NO HOPE

When believers die, the Bible says, they are sleeping....

One of the first-century churches worried about some of their family and friends who had died. They feared that somehow their loved ones had missed the boat and wouldn't be resurrected. Paul wrote to reassure them: *Brothers and sisters, we do not want you to be uninformed about those who sleep in death, so that you do not grieve like the rest of mankind, who have no hope* (1 Thessalonians 4:13).

Believers are not dead, but their bodies are sleeping. The people who inhabited those bodies are with God. In fact, they're doing better than you and I are! But there's something else in that verse that most people gloss over. Look at the last phrase: *who have no hope*. This idea is not a one-off in the Bible; it's the Bible's central theme. Know God, know hope; no God, no hope.

God says that those living without Him *have no future hope* (Proverbs 24:20). Most believers remember all too clearly "*that time [before faith when] you were separate from Christ... **without hope and without God** in the world*" (Ephesians 2:12). But the message to those individuals who belong to God is different: "*I know the plans I have for you," declares the* LORD, "*plans to prosper you and not harm you, plans to give you hope and a future*" (Jeremiah 29:11).

As we come to the end of this book, we arrive at this solid and life-changing, eternity-changing conclusion: Real hope—a hope that changes everything—exists only when we know and trust the true and living God. Jesus said it best when He defined eternal life: "***This** is eternal life, that they may **know You**, the only true God, and Jesus Christ who You have sent*" (John 17:3). The New International Encyclopedia of Words offers this point: "In a most basic way, then, *hope* is a relational term. It is a great affirmation of trust in God, not because the believer knows what is ahead, but because God is known as wholly trustworthy… The [Bible] never shifts from the conviction that relationship with God is the ultimate ground of hope."[54]

EPIC Hope exists. It is real, and it changes everything. But only those who trust and know the living God find and experience this hope. Friends, this is not *my* message. I didn't make this up. I'm only repeating what the Bible and historic Christianity teach. If you don't have a personal relationship with Jesus and with God, then you… have… no… hope in this life. All your so-called hopes are nothing more than self-manufactured wishes that begin and end in your own mind. Tragic.

Now, lest you think I've turned on you, that I'm actually a cold, narrow-minded religious nut, please consider a few things. Why did I wake up at 4:30 a.m., five days a week, and work on this book for three hours a day for 10 months straight? I did it for you, dummy! If you're already a believer and a member of the fam, then you're blessed, and I hope this book has blessed you. But if you haven't noticed yet, I didn't really write this book with Christians in mind as my primary audience. I've labored over this book for those readers who have yet to believe. That is where my heart is, friends. And whether you are a Christian, whatever you believe, if you've made it this far, then you and I have traveled quite a journey together, and I consider you a friend.

If you are that person who, tragically, has no real hope, that can change. Jesus Himself—the living God—invites you to turn to Him:

> *"Come to Me, all you who are weary and burdened, and I will give you rest."* (Matthew 11:28)

---

54 New International Encyclopedia of Bible Words (Grand Rapids, MI: Zondervan, 1985), 343-344.

"I am the resurrection and the life. He who believes in Me, though he may die, he shall live. And whoever lives and believes in Me shall never die. Do you believe this?" (John 11:25-26)

Do you believe this? Jesus asks this question of every person who turns to Him.

Do *you* believe that Jesus is the resurrection and the life?

CHAPTER 18

FINAL THOUGHTS

THIS IS A book about hope. Real, objective hope. My aim for this book was to bring comfort to the downcast and answers to the seeker and the skeptic. My goal was to build a case for true, objective hope, a lifeline that I think is only possible with a foundational Christian understanding of God. I call it EPIC Hope.

In **PART ONE: *WHY WE HOPE,*** I spoke to you from the heart about the wheels of my life falling off and the subsequent several years when I lived—no, when I existed—broken, confused, and depressed. I went through all this even though I knew God and knew a lot about Him. Yet, as I look back, I see that I had some misconceptions about God and about myself, and this wrong thinking harmed me. But God is good, He was always with me, and through the hard times, He taught me to see life anew and become stronger. I also shared with you about my journey with Rebekah and gave you a glimpse of her trials.

So, together, you and I have seen the nature and the necessity of hope. We are hope-hungry creatures who can't live without hope. We also explored the different types of hope—Mundane, Moderate, and Mega—and learned that no matter who they are or what they believe, every person has these hopes. But we came to the realization that all these hopes reduce down to nothing more than self-manufactured wishes that start and end in our heads.

Finally, we saw that God made us human beings in His image and that our hearts instinctively cry out for Someone big and powerful to help us and rescue us. In other words, each one of us is in search of God and a savior. God is by nature independent and self-sufficient *in Himself;* but we are by nature dependent and insufficient *in ourselves.* We are *designed* to need God.

In **PART TWO:** *WHEN OUR HOPES DISAPPOINT,* we spent a good deal of time familiarizing ourselves with our culture's popular hopes, and we saw that each one fails to give real hope and to meet our true heart's needs (The Big Five). I asked several times throughout this discussion, *What if there is another kind of hope that changes everything?* We then got to know a little better the true and living God who is, in fact, knowable as well as transcendent and immanent. Those are necessary prerequisites to objective hope and only the God revealed in Scripture possesses these characteristics.

In **PART THREE:** *HOW TO KNOW REAL HOPE,* I brought into our conversation the most controversial Person in human history: Jesus of Nazareth. I showed how transcendence and immanence merged in the Incarnation: the Word became flesh. Jesus Christ is God incarnate, sent to this world by His loving Father to atone for our sin and bring home His *own special people* (1 Peter 2:9).

Then I attempted to show you how this EPIC Hope changes everything in my life and Rebekah's.

> (1) *I am not alone.* God is always with me. God can reach me and speak to me where no other human can: in my heart of hearts. God is there, and He is not silent.

(2) *A Grand Narrative is in play, and I get to play a special part in it.* In some amazing way, I get to co-author the Story with God. My life and my story are important and meaningful because of Him.

(3) *Suffering has meaning and purpose.* We don't always know why we struggle and suffer, but the super cool part is that we don't need to always know why. What we do know and can find confidence in is that our trials always have meaning and purpose, and they often play a central role in developing our stories and fulfilling our life purpose. We can trust the One who knows the meaning and purpose of our suffering.

(4) *I'm deeply loved.* God loves *me!* And it's not just because of Jesus or what Jesus did. God also doesn't just love me only when I'm performing well or just because of what I can do for Him. God loves me just because. Period. And God loves me for me so much so that He sacrificed His only beloved Son so that He could make a way for me to be in relationship with Him. Jesus, too, loves me so much that He willingly died for me. The cross of Christ is the greatest demonstration of God's love for me... and for you.

(5) *Jesus's death and resurrection defeated public enemy #1: death.* Because Jesus lives, we can live. God offers the gift of eternal life to anyone who believes the gospel and follows Jesus. Furthermore, believers can even now celebrate this amazing truth: *I have eternal life right now! I will never die!*

CONCLUSION

KNOW—AND I PLANNED—THAT the farther you traveled into this book, the more theological it got. The forest got denser with each chapter, and I hope I've proven a genuine and trustworthy guide for you. When writing a book, you always want to keep your audience in mind. Most of my current friends are Christians, but I rarely had them or any other Christian in mind when I wrote this. Though if you are a Christian reading this, I'm grateful, and I hope you've benefited. But as I wrote this book, I felt as if I were always talking to you who have yet to believe, you who are on the fence, you who think you know God but really don't, you who feel hopeless and lost in this crazy world, you who feel like you have no reason to live, you who are hurting and afraid, and, yes, even you who thinks all this God stuff is phony bologna.

I want you—whoever you are—to realize that everything I've said in this book is real to me. It's not a game or a theory or a tradition. I really believe this, and it's my life. For better or worse, I live this every day.

I opened the previous chapter by saying that I think about death a lot. I shared with you some reasons why, but there's another reason, one intimately close to me: my wife. Rebekah has stage 4 metastatic breast cancer. Apart from God or a medical miracle performed by God, there is no cure. As I write this, she is doing well with treatments, even winning, but the typical life expectancy rates are not encouraging. My previous books go into detail about the difficulties of this journey, but what I want you to see is that we are in the trenches of this life-and-death battle every day. Cancer or alcohol or fear or despair—all this is part of our story right now. We've had in the past and we will continue to receive heartbreaking news and have excruciating conversations as death keeps trying to take her.

Yet, despite all that Rebekah and I are facing, we live with deep joy and genuine hope! These various issues have struck us down but not destroyed us. Because we have an EPIC Hope, we've learned to get back up and stand strong after life knocks us down. Sometimes standing is all you can do and even all you need to do: when you pick yourself up and stand again, you demonstrate immense strength and power. Life and the world and our biology have thrown bombs of sh#t at Rebekah and me, yet we stand. There's blood. Yet we stand. There're tears. Yet we stand. There's dread. Yet we stand. There's sorrow. Yet we stand. There's anger. Yet we stand. But we stand only because our King stands. And He stands after going through His own journey of pain and sorrow. Yet He stands. He stands *with* us and He stands *for* us. And, friend, He stands in power and might, in mercy and love. Without this EPIC Hope, Rebekah and I both admit, we would not be here today.

To you who already believe in the true and living God, these same benefits and blessings are yours! Rejoice and give thanks!

To you who have yet to make that faith commitment, what are you waiting for? Your Creator is waiting for you with open arms. The One who formed you in your mother's womb, the One who sustains your life, the One who keeps your heart beating, the One who upholds all that exists says, "Come to Me for life. Come to Me for EPIC Hope" (see Isaiah 55:1-3).

This is an open invitation now. It expires when we exhale our last breath. I came to God around 18 or 19 years of age. For me, it's changed everything. My dad barely made it in time. Many never make it at all.

Because of who God is and because of what Jesus did, we can bring to Him all our hopes—Mundane, Moderate, Mega, whatever!—and we can experience inner peace knowing that He loves us.

EPIC Hope *transcends* all human desires, designs, and devisings because it comes to us from outside time and space. It's supernatural. It's God.

EPIC Hope *lifts* us up and above our circumstances because it helps us see everything from the perspective of God who is in complete control of all of human history and all of your story.

EPIC Hope *baptizes* and *covers* all our desires and plans by giving them eternal significance.

EPIC Hope *yields confident expectations* because it tells us about the future with absolute certainty. We believers can't know everything about how our personal plans will unfold, but we can know a lot:

- God loves me, cares for me, and will never leave or forsake me.

- God is sovereign: He is in complete control of everything, even the awful things.

- God is good, and He will always do what is good and right.

- God forgave all my sins, and I can come to Him anytime with absolute confidence He will welcome me.

- I have eternal life right now and forever. I didn't earn it, and I can never lose it.

- To be absent from my body means I will be present with the Lord.

- Someday God will resurrect the basic elements of my body, recreate it in a new and glorified form, and then reunite it with my soul.

- Someday God will right every wrong, and all evil will be conquered by the divine justice it deserves.

- I will dwell with the Lord forever.[55]

And this list is only a sample of the truths we know about now and the future. The main takeaway is this: no matter what happens in this life, we can ALWAYS have hope. In this life, we will experience some setbacks, and we'll lose some battles ("God, grant me the serenity..."), but we know how the Story ends: we win.

Situations where we need hope—the Mundane, the Moderate, and even the Mega—come and go, but EPIC Hope is always there, always fueled by God's love, and always enfolding our common hopes because God cares about even our smallest issues. Because God cares about us as individuals who feel, who desire, who hurt. Because God cares about our hearts.

---

55 These Scriptures are listed in the same order as the bulleted statements they support: Romans 5:8; Hebrews 13:5; Genesis 50:20; James 1:17; 1 Peter 1:15; Psalm 103:12; Hebrews 4:16-18; Ephesians 2:8-10; Philippians 1:6; John 10:27-29; 2 Corinthians 5:6-8; 1 Corinthians 15:35-58; Romans 8:28-30; 2 Corinthians 5:10; Matthew 25:31-46; Revelation 21:4; Psalm 23:6.

And so we come to the end. I will step aside and leave you here with Jesus. You two may have some things to talk about. Don't worry. Notice His smile. See that His arms are open. He's waited a long time for this. He's waited a long time for *you*.

THE BIG FIVE

Ultimately, we want to know the following:

- **WE ARE NOT ALONE.** We want to know that there is Someone Big out there who listens, who cares, and who can actually do something—even something miraculous—to help.

- **LIFE HAS MEANING.** We want to know that life is not pointless; that we really matter; and that life has an ultimate meaning that gives us purpose on this earth.

- **SUFFERING HAS PURPOSE.** We want to know that loss, sorrow, hardship, trials, and pain are not pointless, that something good can come out of our dark times even if the circumstances don't resolve the way we want them to.

- **WE CAN FIND THE POWER.** We want to know that we can find inner comfort, strength, and peace that will get us through Mega storms.

- **THERE IS LIFE AFTER DEATH:** We want to know that, when we die physically, somehow we don't cease to exist; somehow we will live on after death; and wherever we are living will be a better place.

MISCONCEPTIONS ABOUT EPIC HOPE

Knowing God and having EPIC Hope will change *everything*. But I need to clarify two popular misconceptions about what it means to have EPIC Hope.

FIRST, KNOWING GOD IS NOT A MAGIC SHIELD

Knowing the true and living God does not automatically shield us from struggle, heartbreak, failure, pain, or suffering. Now I do suspect, as the Bible indicates, that being a child of God shields and protects us from numerous personal weaknesses, bad decisions, terrible timings, physical accidents, the evil plots of others, and attacks from demonic hosts. I also believe that in God's providential sovereign care for His kids, He protects us from a multitude of ills and evils that we never even know about. You see, as a child of God I have total confidence that God is *for* me. Check this out:

> *If God is for us, who can be against us? He who did not spare His own Son, but gave Him up for us all—how will He not also, along with Him, graciously give us all things?* (Romans 8:31-32)

Now, consider these scenarios. You need to be somewhere, but you can't find your car keys. It's so frustrating—but what if God is meddling a bit so that you leave the house five minutes later and miss getting t-boned or hitting that kid who runs across the street after a ball? Or what if *not* getting that job that I wanted so bad and that was so perfect for me, was actually God protecting me from a woman there who could have led to the ruin of my family? What if getting fired was really not the worst thing that could have happened even though it seemed that way at the time? What if I hadn't gotten fired but, because of fear, had spent the next 15 years at that stupid job when I should have been doing something else, something better, that God had for me? And what if going through that terrible divorce was actually part of a much bigger plan, a plan for my ultimate good, a plan that would lead to a hundred new blessings, and a plan that I would look back on years later and say, "Thank You, God"?

I also believe that, as the Bible teaches, an unseen spiritual world, another realm of reality, seems to intersect with our own temporal reality. In fact, I believe this world is filled with angelic hosts—some good and some evil. And the idea of having a guardian angel is not foreign to the Bible. So what if being part of God's family means that He's assigned angelic warriors to watch over, guard, and protect us from evils in this world as well as from attacks from the demonic? The Bible talks about this kind of stuff (see Daniel 10; Ephesians 6:10-12). I firmly believe a whole lot more is going on in this world than meets the eye.

I know that God is for me, so I believe that this kind of stuff—this kind of divine intervention, protection, and provision—happens all the time. And I think that's pretty darn cool. But God is *not* a helicopter Parent hovering over us and protecting us from every evil and ill that comes our way. God is a *good* and *wise* and *loving* Father. If He protected us from every potential bug bite, then we'd never mature, never grow, never learn to persevere. Struggle, pain, and suffering yield blessed lessons in how to stand, how to fight, and how to grow. Those valuable lessons are why loving and wise parents sometimes allow their child to fall, fail, and be hurt.

This truth reminds me of a most insightful poem called "The Master Weaver." It is usually attributed to Corrie ten Boom (1892-1983), a Jewish Christian who, as a young girl, not only survived the Nazi Holocaust but also helped many other Jews escape by hiding them in her family home.[56]

> *My life is but a weaving*
> *Between my God and me.*
> *I cannot choose the colors*
> *He weaveth steadily.*
>
> *Oft' times He weaveth sorrow;*
> *And I in foolish pride*
> *Forget He sees the upper*
> *And I the underside.*
>
> *Not 'til the loom is silent*
> *And the shuttle cease to fly*
> *Will God unroll the canvas*
> *And reveal the reason why.*
>
> *The dark threads are as needful*
> *In the Weaver's skillful hand*
> *As the threads of gold and silver*
> *In the pattern He has planned.*

Did you catch that last stanza? "The dark threads are as needful in the Weaver's skillful hand as the threads of gold and silver in

---

56 A movie was made about her life and story called *The Hiding Place* (1975).

the pattern He has planned." As Corrie pointed out, often we only see the underside of the tapestry, the side with all the mess, the tangles, the knots, the random colors, the crisscross threads. We often only see or feel the confusion of those dark threads. But God sees both the under *and* the upper sides as His plan unfolds, and His plan fulfilled will be a beautiful work of art.

Again, knowing God is not a magic shield protecting us from all struggle, failure, pain, and suffering. A good, wise, and loving parent will at times allow such things into our lives to fulfill "the pattern [God] has planned." I think it's really cool that God even refers to each one of us who trust Him as *His poem*. Yeah, check this out: *We are His workmanship* (Ephesians 2:10). That word *workmanship* is the Greek word *poiema* from where we get our English word *poem*. It conveys the idea of something skillfully made by an artist. And you and I were skillfully, exquisitely, intricately made by the divine Artist.

SECOND, KNOWING GOD IS NOT A QUICK FIX

Honestly, I wish it were. Most of the time, I've learned—and I am still learning!—that God likes to take us on the long road to recovery as opposed to delivering a quick fix. After all, God seeks to grow us up into maturity, into strong adults, into men and women who can stand strong and persevere against all—natural and supernatural—that comes our way.

But that's not how God always works! I've learned it's both dangerous and stupid to think we know how God will always work. God is a Master of the unconventional. He will do what seems to us as either foolish or crazy or both—and I suspect He's grinning the whole time. In his excellent book *Walking with God Through Pain and Suffering,* Timothy Keller wrote the following:

The world expects a God who is strong and whose followers are blessed and successful only if they summon up all their strength and follow His laws without fail. That was the view of Job's friends, of the Pharisees in Jesus' day, and, according to Luther, the mind-set of most of the leaders of the medieval church in his day. It was a 'theology of glory," but it was not the theology of the Bible. The Scripture's startling message is rather that the deepest revelation of the character of God is in the weakness, suffering, and death of the cross. This is "the exact opposite of where humanity expected to find God."[57]

In Jesus' day, most of the Jewish leaders expected that when the Messiah appeared, he would be a mighty military leader who would lead a revolution, overthrow Rome, and lead Israel to political independence. These Jewish leaders expected a Messiah who'd be direct and easy to understand. They expected power, might, and force. They expected blood, but not the blood only of the Messiah and surely not His death. Because of these wrong expectations, they couldn't see Jesus for who He was. Even Jesus' own disciples—who did believe He was the Messiah—couldn't fathom the idea that He was going to die and rise again even though the Old Testament had predicted it and even though Jesus Himself had often told them.

Next, let's think together about Job from the Old Testament. Job suffered sudden calamities and immeasurable loss in his personal life. Job's friends thought they understood what God was up to: Job was a rotten tomato who was being punished for deep, dark, hidden sin in his life. But such was not at all the case. In reality, Job was an upright man who trusted God. "Job's sufferings were actually quite mysterious, and God's purposes were hidden from Job and most of them even from the book's readers," says Keller.

---

57 Keller, 50.

"And yet out of Job's agony and suffering came one of the most profound revelations of God's nature in the Bible and indeed in all of literature—as well as a transformed character for Job."[58]

Now let's think about Jesus on the cross. Again, Keller has great insight:

> Those looking at Jesus as He was dying on the cross had no idea that they were looking at the greatest act of salvation in history. Could the observers of the crucifixion "clearly perceive" the ways of God? No—even though they were looking right at a wonder of grace. They saw only darkness and pain, and the categories of human reason are sure God cannot be working in and through that.[59]

You've undoubtedly had that same thought: "God cannot be working in and through *that*." Imagine the people standing around the cross, their hands over their mouths in disbelief. Imagine them pointing at the broken man covered in blood, flesh torn, most likely naked, utterly defeated, and hanging in disgrace on a Roman cross. God cannot be working in *that!* God *cannot*... Yet God was indeed carrying out the most profound plan in all of human history, and everyone missed it.[60]

> Only through weakness and pain did God save us and show us, in the deepest way possible, the infinite depths of His grace and love for us. For indeed, here was infinite wisdom—in one stroke, the just requirement of the law was fulfilled and the forgiveness of lawbreakers secured. In one moment, God's love and justice were fully satisfied. This

---

58 Ibid., 51.
59 Ibid., 51.
60 Everyone missed it except for some of the women who followed Jesus. These women seemed to have a greater insight into who Jesus really was than their male counterparts did. No wonder Jesus had a special place in His heart for women who had long been silenced and oppressed in ancient Jewish culture.

Messiah came to die in order to put an end to death itself.
Only through weakness and suffering could sin be atoned—
it was the only way to end evil without ending us.61

We need to tread carefully when we think we know how God works in our lives and in the lives of others. Knowing God doesn't guarantee quick fixes to our problems. Sometimes a quick fix happens, but not always. The world of Christendom is replete with stories of immediate deliverance and dramatic rescue. While I've experienced some big deliverances in my own life, most of my journey has felt like a struggle.

God saved me when I was around the age of 18 or 19. One of my best friends at the time felt God calling him back to his faith, so he completely left our whole scene. He started going to church, and his life changed dramatically. He invited me to go to church with him. After several invites, I finally joined him. My conversion didn't immediately come about because of a lightning bolt from God; it unfolded over a period of weeks and months. But I distinctly remember being consciously aware of hearing/sensing/feeling God call me to come "out of the world" and to go to Him. It was something that I just knew—and something that I knew had to happen. I remember feeling as if my time in the world was coming to an end and that a new chapter was about to begin in my life. I'm using the word *world* the way the Bible does: I'm referring to the world systems and world's attitudes that—whether manifesting as a quiet indifference or a violent protest—are against the true and living God. Today we call it **agnosticism** or *secular humanism*.

Later, after I became a Christian, I read a portion of the Bible that confirmed this inner voice and call that I was hearing. Jesus said, *"My sheep hear My voice, and I know them, and they*

---
61 Keller, 51.

follow Me. And I give them eternal life, and they shall never perish" (John 10:27-28).

Now, remember, we're talking about the fact that knowing God doesn't mean a quick fix to all our problems, that God doesn't always work the same way, and that, while radical and immediate deliverance is not the norm, God does do it. He did it with me and my drinking. Actually, He did it with a lot of things for me! I also saw God radically and immediately deliver many of my hoodlum friends who came to faith.

After I finally came to faith in Christ, I just stopped drinking. It wasn't a struggle. I didn't have to fight it. I just didn't care anymore. I had found something—better stated, I had found Someone—far greater and more attractive than partying or getting drunk. I also quit smoking. That one was a battle, but still God gave me the strength, power, ability—whatever you want to call it—to quit. I also quit cussing, quit racism, quit anger, quit perversion, and quit being a jerk. My whole perspective on life had changed because I had a revolutionary change in my world-view. I saw God, the world, people, and myself in a whole new way: God had given me an eternal perspective. Life now had real and objective meaning, purpose, and value! I saw beauty for the first time. God's Word says, *With You [God] is the fountain of life; in Your light we see light* (Psalm 36:9). I had a joy and excitement about life that I had never known.

God delivered me from something I never thought I'd be free of. Maybe that's the point. Maybe I needed to realize that I couldn't get free in my own power: *"With man this is impossible, but with God all things are possible"* (Matthew 19:26). From age 20 to age 30, I never had a single drink of alcohol or a cigarette. I never even thought about it. Never once during those years did I ever feel a single urge to resort to either of those coping devices. Those were dead remnants from a past life... until...

THE WHIP PULLS ME BACK

Bear with me as I bring in another *Lord of the Rings* analogy. A few days ago, our close friend Valerie came by to say hi and catch up a little. Seeing *The Lord of the Rings* DVD case on the table, she said that when the first movie came out, she saw it with her son. She really enjoyed it, but she was upset by the abrupt ending. (It really does leave you hanging, but it's a strong setup for the second movie.) Valerie said that she was so upset by the ending that she never saw the remaining two movies! Can you believe that? Yeah, I thought it was crazy too. These are the greatest movies ever made, and she hasn't seen them! If you, dear reader, are like Valerie, your homework *this weekend* is to have a *Lord of the Rings* party. (Valerie, I know you will read this book at some point. You need to watch those movies!) Okay, I just had to get that off my chest.

Now, if you remember from the first movie, in the deep cave of Moria, Gandalf the wizard fights a powerful demon called Balrog in the Battle of the Peak. As they battle on a narrow stone bridge suspended above a most treacherous drop, Balrog fights with a long whip of flaming fire. In the movie, Gandalf slams down his staff and says his famous line: "You... shall... not... pass!" Balrog is stunned, but then he charges Gandalf. As he does, the bridge collapses under his enormous weight. Balrog falls into the darkness. It's done. It's over. Gandalf won. But as Gandalf turns to join his friends, Balrog's whip lashes up and grabs Gandalf's ankle, pulling him to the edge where eventually he falls into the same darkness into which Balrog had fallen. Gandalf's friends—the hobbits and the men—think he is dead, and the first movie ends.

But we learn in the second movie that Gandalf is far from dead. In the movie we see him battling Balrog as they fall all the way down. They eventually end up on a mountain peak called Silverstine. There they fought for two days and nights "until at last I threw down my enemy and smote his ruin upon the mountainside" (Gandalf).[62]

I see this battle between Gandalf and Balrog as a picture of the Christian life, of my life at least. After ten years of total sobriety, I felt the whip of my old enemy grab my ankle and pull me down. Like Gandalf in his moment of apparent victory, I never expected to see that demon again. It took Gandalf two days and nights of fierce fighting, no doubt getting bloodied himself, until he finally smote Balrog on the mountainside. My fight has lasted me ten years. I've had victories, and I've been bloodied. My faith in God has been beaten-the-hell-up, yet it is stronger now than it ever was when I was in my twenties.

My thirties were a battleground: I'd get crushed, and I struggled to learn to stand. During my twenties, faith and life came easy. Looking back, my faith felt like a game, and I was good at the game. God gave me a lot of grace, and it functioned like the fuel and the rockets on the space shuttle. For ten years, God's grace shot me into space, to the heavens. But just as it happens on the space shuttle, the fuel ran dry and the rockets fell off. I found myself alone, naked, and floating aimlessly in space, struggling for direction and gasping for oxygen. I longed for the days of old when I had plenty of fuel and was full of fire.

But as my faith in God got beat up, it strangely grew stronger. And I think the strength came because my faith and my Jesus were all I had. When you and I are on Easy Street, we don't pay attention, we get lazy with our faith, and we take a lot for

---

62 You can watch this on YouTube: "Lord of the Rings - Gandalf vs Balrog."

granted. But when we're in the grip of an existential crisis, we think more clearly, we get laser focused, and we reevaluate what matters most in life. Crisis strips away the fluff and fakeness, and it forces the ruthless and painful examination of ourselves and of everything we believe.

Then, in the latter part of my thirties, I learned how to stand again, but everything was different. Christianity and life were no longer a game. Rather than winning or losing, I realized you just keep pushing the heck forward. My faith took hits, but it stood. The truths I know came under question, but they carried me through. Sometimes I was barely crawling, but I was crawling forward nonetheless. I feel that I became not only more mature in my faith but also more empathetic, more patient, more merciful, more... real.

I'm now 42. I look back on my twenties with great appreciation for all that fuel and those many rockets. I look back on my thirties, and I'm equally thankful—maybe more so—for the struggles, the failures, the pain, and the suffering.

We human beings want quick fixes, immediate deliverance, and we'll pray for those. Sometimes God answers our prayer, and we praise Him for His rapid response—and rightly so. More often, though, because He is a good, wise, and loving Father, He lets us sweat and struggle so that we come to know Him better and He can teach us to stand. If we look at our trials—those times of floating alone in space, struggling for direction and for oxygen—in this light, maybe we'll realize that those times are also gifts of grace and God's care. And maybe this is the kind of situation the apostle James was referring to when he wrote these rather bewildering words:

> *Consider it pure joy, my brothers and sisters, whenever you face trials of many kinds,* because you know *that the testing of your faith produces perseverance. Let perseverance finish its work so that you may be mature and complete, not lacking anything.* (James 1:2-4)

This truth makes me think of Laura Story's beautiful song "Blessings." I encourage you to listen to it. You can find it on YouTube.

GLOSSARY OF TERMS USED IN THIS BOOK

*Each term in the glossary has been made **bold** at its first occurrence in the book's text.*

Adam and Eve: The first man and woman created by God. The Bible, including Jesus, take Adam and Eve as real, historical people who lived in a geographic location called Eden.

Agnosticism: A person who claims not to know, or thinks it is impossible to know, whether there is a God.

Allah: The God of the religion, Islam.

Angst: Angst refers to a type of anxiety. Angst is that deep, under-lying, unsettling, never-restful feeling that something is wrong and that *that* something will get worse, not better. It's that painful existential feeling of incompleteness and emptiness.

Apologetics: A branch of theology that deals with the vindication of the Christian philosophy of life (i.e. the Bible) against the various forms of non-Christian philosophy of life. It answers and offers both defensive and offensive arguments.

Apostle John: One of the twelve apostles of Jesus. John wrote five books in the New Testament, including the Gospel according to John and the book of Revelation.

Apostle Paul: One of Jesus's later apostles (after the resurrection). Paul taught the Gospel to both Jews and Gentiles in the first century. He wrote 13 (maybe 14) of the 27 books of the New Testament.

Apostle Peter: One of Jesus's twelve apostles and a leader in the early church. Peter wrote two books in the New Testament and supplied testimony for one of the gospel accounts.

Atheism: A person who believes there is no God.

Atonement: The work Christ did in His life and death to earn our salvation.

Big Questions: Literally, "self-law," or "self-rule." Human autonomy asserts that man's reasoning is free from God and is the ultimate criterion of truth, justice, morals, and meaning.

Bible: Believed by many people throughout history to be the divinely inspired revelation from God to man. The Bible comprises 66 books (or scrolls), written over about 4,000 years, by over 40 authors. It is divided by the Old Testament (39 books) and the New Testament (27 books).

Big Questions: By this I mean the big questions of life: Where did everything come from? Does God exist? What's the meaning of life? How to we determine right from wrong? Is there life after death? Etc.

Buddhism: A faith that was founded by Siddhartha Gautama ("the Buddha") more than 2,500 years ago in India.

Chance (Accident): The idea that events happen on their own without any intelligent or rational cause.

Christ: The central figure of Christianity. Christians believe Christ is their Savior and their God. *Christ* is from a Greek word that harkens back to the Old Testament word for Messiah. Christ is not Jesus's last name. Jesus is *the* Christ (i.e. Messiah).

Christian: A person who believes that the Bible is the inspired Word of God and also believes the central historical doctrines of the Bible. A Christian is someone who trusts in the grace of God alone for their salvation, apart from any and all works.

Creation: The teaching that God created the entire universe out of nothing.

Deism: A type of natural religion which was very prevalent in the 17th and 18th centuries. Deists hold that God can be discovered and proven from reason alone apart from any special revelation. The God of deism created the world, but does not interfere with it.

Despair: The complete loss or absence of hope.

Divine Inspiration: Meaning literally "God-breathed" (from 2 Tim. 3:16), and referring to the divinely authoritative writings of Holy Scripture, which God produced without destroying the individual styles of the writers.

Doctrine: What the whole Bible teaches on a particular topic (e.g. angels, death, etc.).

Dualism: Dualism holds that there are two ultimate realities, usually seen as mind and matter or good and evil.

Empirical: Knowledge that is observational, relying on sense perception. It is guided by experience rather than theory.

Enlightenment: The European (secular) intellectual movement of the 17th and 18th centuries in which ideas concerning God, reason, nature, and man were blended into a worldview that lead to revolutionary ideas in philosophy, art, and politics. The term *Enlightenment* was coined to contrast with the supposed Dark Ages, when the universities were largely controlled by the church.

Epic: A long narrative poem written in elevated style, in which heroes of great historical or legendary importance perform valorous deeds. The setting is vast in scope, covering great nations, the world, or the universe, and the action is important to the history of a nation or people.

Ethics: The branch of philosophy known as moral philosophy. It studies right and wrong attitudes, judgments, and actions, as well as moral responsibility and obligation.

ex nihilo: Latin phrase meaning "out of nothing," referring to God's creation of the universe without using any preexisting materials.

Existential: Relating to and dealing with moment by moment human existence.

Existentialism: A modern theory of philosophy that holds that human experience is not describable in scientific or rational terms. Existentialism stresses the need to make vital choices by using man's freedom in an apparently purposeless world.

Faith: Trust or dependence on God and what He has said in His Word.

Finite: Having limits or bounds.

Gospel: Literally, "good news" or "good story." The Christian Gospel is the good news about the life, death, resurrection, and ascension of Jesus Christ.

Grace: God, giving us what we don't deserve. Grace is God's goodness toward those who deserve only punishment.

Grand Narrative: The grand eternal plan of God.

Greek Philosophers: Ancient Greek philosophy arose in the 6th century BC and continued throughout the Hellenistic period and the period. Historians often make distinctions with *pre*-Socratic thinkers (those before Socrates), and the Socratics (Socrates, Plato, Aristotle).

Heart: The Bible uses the word "heart" holistically to represent our entire self: our mind, our emotions, our beliefs, and our will.

Heaven: The Bible uses this word in several ways. Particularly, it speaks of "the heavens," meaning the sky or space. Some biblical writers also use this word to refer to the dwelling place of God or the eternal realm where angels and believers will spend eternity with God. It is described as a place of glory.

Hell: A place of eternal conscious torment for the wicked.

Holiness (Perfection): The teaching that God is separated from sin.

Hope: A personal confidence and assurance of what God has done, is doing, and will do in the future.

Image of God: The special nature of human beings that makes them like God and distinct from the animal world.

Immanent: Existing or remaining in. The term refers to God's active involvement in His creation.

Incarnation: Incarnation derives from the Latin *incarnare*, "to become flesh." In Christian theology it refers to the coming of the invisible, spiritual God in bodily form in Jesus Christ.

Inductive Reasoning: Looking to or using previous experience(s) to forecast or predict future outcomes. I've enjoyed Taco Bell 99% of the time before, I will probably enjoy it today.

Infinite: Without limits or boundaries. When used of God, it means God is not subject to any of the limitations of humanity or of creation in general.

Justice: Another term for God's righteousness, meaning God must always does what is right and good.

Lewis, C. S.: Clive Staples Lewis (1898–1963) was one of the intellectual giants of the twentieth century and arguably one of the most influential writers of his day. He wrote more than 30 books.

Luther, Martin: (1483-1546). A leader in what we now call the Protestant Reformation. Luther attempted to pull the German Catholic Church back to the Bible and so precipitated the Protestant break with Roman Catholicism.

Materialism (Naturalism): Materialism is a presupposition that believes everything in existence is reducible to material or physical properties. Materialists deny things like God, souls, spirits, minds, angels, etc. Naturalism is the philosophical belief that everything arises from natural properties and causes, and supernatural or spiritual explanations are excluded or discounted.

Mercy: God not giving us what we deserve (i.e. judgment).

Messiah: An Old Testament teaching that God would send a final Prophet and Savior to deliver His people from sin and struggle.

Mindfulness: A mental state achieved by focusing one's awareness on the present moment, while calmly acknowledging and accepting one's feelings, thoughts, and bodily sensations, used as a therapeutic technique.

Nacho Libre: One of the funniest movies ever (after Napoleon Dynamite).

New Age (Spiritualism): Usually called "spiritualism" nowadays, the New Age Movement is a hodgepodge of anything and everything mystical, from energy crystals, witchcraft, and aliens to Buddhist principles, massage therapy, and acupuncture. New Age spirituality holds to a pantheistic view of God and reality.

New Testament: The sacred writings of Christianity and the second part of the Christian Bible. Christians see the New Testament as the fulfillment of the Old Testament writings and prophecies. New Testament is not to be confused with the new covenant, though they are similar.

Objective: Something not influenced by personal feelings or opinions. Used in contrast to subjective feelings or opinions. Something is objective if it has a public nature and is right or true, regardless of differing opinions.

Old Testament: The sacred writings of Judaism and the first part of the Christian Bible. Christians hold the Old Testament as equally sacred and inspired as the New Testament, and they see the New Testament as the fulfillment of the Old Testament prophecies. Old Testament is not to be confused with the old covenant, though they are similar.

Omniscience: Refers to the teaching that God fully knows himself and all things actual and possible in one simple and eternal act. God is all-knowing.

Omnipotence: Refers to God's ability to do all that He wills. God is all-powerful.

Omnipresence: Refers to God's personal, simultaneous presence everywhere throughout the created universe. God is always ever present.

Oncology: A branch of medicine that deals with the prevention, diagnosis, and treatment of cancer.

Ontology: A branch of philosophy (metaphysics) that deals with the nature of being or existence.

Pantheism: The idea or belief that God and Nature are identical. The universe is seen as an extension of God's essence rather than a special creation from God.

Philosophy: Literally, "the love of wisdom." Philosophy is the attempt to think rationally and critically about the Big Questions of life. The main branches of philosophy are: metaphysics, epistemology, ethics, aesthetics, logic, and mind.

Prayer: Personal communication with God.

Presupposition: A basic (or foundational) assumption in one's reasoning or in the process by which opinions are formed. It differs from ordinary assumptions in that a presupposition is a core-belief about the nature of reality, knowledge, and ethics. Presuppositions are the starting points of our worldviews and thus determine how we see and interpret everything in life.

Propositional Revelation: The God-revealed words of the Bible that make up sentences and give us true knowledge about God and life.

Providence: Literally, "to see beforehand." Providence is the teaching that God is continually involved with all created things in causing, directing, and sustaining them to fulfill His purposes.

Psalms: A book in the Old Testament comprising 150 musical or poetic expressions.

Reality: Metaphysics is a branch of philosophy that studies the origin, structure, and nature of ultimate reality. Metaphysics asks questions like, *Where did everything come from? What is everything ultimately made of? What controls or causes everything in our experience?*

Redemption: A term used to describe Christ's work of "buying back" sinners out of their bondage to sin and Satan through the payment of a ransom (Himself).

Reformation: The **Protestant Reformation** was a major 16th century European movement aimed initially at reforming the beliefs and practices of the Roman Catholic Church. Its most notable characters are Martin Luther, John Calvin, and Ulrich Zwingli.

Relativism (Moral): An ethical philosophy that holds that since there are no universal absolutes binding on all people, morality is relative to the individual.

Resurrection: In Christianity, resurrection refers to the rising from the dead (physically) into a new kind of life not subject to sickness, aging, deterioration, or death.

Revelation: The act of God disclosing or revealing objectively true aspects of Himself to His creation. Theologians make a distinction between *general* revelation and *special* revelation. General revelation is God's communication to all people, regardless of belief. This includes, among others, the wonders of creation, acts of goodness through providence, and human conscience as image bearers. Special revelation is God communicating to humanity through His verbally inspired, propositional revelation, or what we call the Bible.

Saved: A biblical term referring to a lost sinner who has received forgiveness of sins and eternal life through Jesus Christ. Jesus spoke of this as being "born again."

Schaeffer, Francis A. (1912-1984). Presbyterian missionary to Europe and the intellectuals of the West. Most responsible for sparking a revival of evangelical intellectual and social responsibility in the twentieth century.

Scripture: A term used by biblical writers that refers to the verbally inspired writings.

Secularism (Humanism): A worldview that believes the here and now is all that exists. Secularism and secular humanism deny any transcendent God or afterlife. Secular humanism and atheism go hand-in-hand.

Sin (evil): Any failure to conform to the moral law of God in act, attitude, or nature.

Skepticism: Skepticism says we do not know anything for certain. All knowledge is at best probable or nothing more than opinion.

Soul (spirit or mind): The immaterial part of man. Used interchangeably in the Bible with spirit and mind.

Sovereign: God's complete exercise of power over His creation.

Spirit (God's or Holy Spirit): In the Bible, "God's Spirit" or the "Spirit of God" usually refers to the third Person of the Trinity, the Holy Spirit. The Holy Spirit is co-eternal and co-equal with God the Father and God the Son.

Subjective: Ideas, opinions, or beliefs based on a person's feelings, experience, preference, or personal beliefs.

Supernatural: Used in contrast to *natural* and *naturalism.* Supernatural refers to any action or realm outside our natural world and experience.

Taco Bell: A place that makes many people very, very happy.

The Big Five: The five primary desires every human has, as I see it. See Appendix 1.

***The Lord of the Rings* (trilogy):** The greatest movie trilogy ever made.

Theology: From two Greek words meaning the study of God.

Time/Space Continuum: In physics, space-time is any mathematical model which fuses the three dimensions of space and the one dimension of time into a single four-dimensional manifold.

Transcendent: A term used to describe God as being greater than His creation and independent (or outside) of it.

Trinity: The teaching that God eternally exists as three Persons—the Father, the Son, and the Holy Spirit—and each Person is fully God and comprises the One true God.

Truth: Statements and concepts that are objectively true independent of human opinion.

Worldview: A network of presuppositions about reality, knowledge, and conduct by which we interpret and understand the world. A worldview is the unique way each person "sees" God, the world, and people, including themselves.

Yahweh: The most revered and most personal name of God in the Old Testament. Also known as the Tetragrammaton because it is composed of four Hebrew letters. Jesus claimed to be Yahweh incarnate.

A SHORT LIST OF RECOMMENDED READING

The following books are a short list of books *I personally recommend*. This list could, of course, span the length of the book in your hands. But each of these books have made significant impacts on my life at some point in my journey, many of them I return to over and over as needed such as those by Francis Schaeffer and John Eldredge. These are some of the heroes of my faith.

For Skeptics

- *The God who is There,* Francis A. Schaeffer.

- *He is There and He is Not Silent,* Francis A. Schaeffer.

- *Christianity Considered,* John Frame.

- *More Than A Carpenter,* Josh McDowell.

For New Believers

- *More Than A Carpenter,* Josh McDowell.

- *Crazy Love,* Francis Chan.

- *Essential Truths of the Christian Faith*, R. C. Sproul.

For Hope and Encouragement

- *Comforts from the Cross*, Elyse M. Fitzpatrick.

- *Because He Loves Me*, Elyse M. Fitzpatrick.

- *New Morning Mercies*, Paul David Tripp.

For Pain and Suffering

- *Walking with God through Pain and Suffering*, Timothy Keller.

- *Where Is God When It Hurts?* Philip Yancey.

- *Streams in the Deserts*, L. B. Cowman, edited by Jim Reimann.

- *Counsel from The Cross*, Elyse M. Fitzpatrick.

Christian Living and Discipleship

- All books by John Eldredge.

- *Love Your God with All Your Mind*, J. P. Moreland.

- *True Spirituality*, Francis A. Schaeffer.

- All books by Donald Miller.

Devotional

- *Comforts from the Cross*, Elyse M. Fitzpatrick.

- *New Morning Mercies*, Paul David Tripp.

- *Streams in the Deserts*, L. B. Cowman, edited by Jim Reimann

Theology

- *Systematic Theology,* Wayne Grudem.

- *Knowing God,* J. I. Packer.

- *Is God Really in Control?* Jerry Bridges.

Jesus

- *Crazy Love,* Francis Chan.

- *More Jesus, Less Religion,* Stephen Arterburn and Jack Felton.

- *Jesus the King,* Timothy Keller.

History

- *How Should We Then Live,* Francis A. Schaeffer.

- *The Meaning of History,* Ronald H. Nash.

- *The New Evidence That Demands A Verdict,* Josh McDowell.

- *Archaeology and Bible History,* Joseph P. Free.

Bible

- *Living by the Book,* Howard Hendricks and William Hendricks.

- *A General Introduction to the Bible,* Norman Geisler and William E. Nix.

- *God, Revelation, and Authority,* Carl F. H. Henry (Advanced).

Apologetics/Philosophy/Worldviews

- *Pushing the Antithesis,* Greg. L. Bahnsen, edited by Gary DeMar.

- *The Universe Next Door,* James W. Sire.

- *A Christian View of Men and Things,* Gordon H. Clark.

- *Every Thought Captive,* Richard L. Pratt, Jr.

- *Science and Its Limits,* Del Ratzsch.

- *The Death of Truth,* Dennis McCallum.

- *The Transforming Vision,* Brian J. Walsh and J. Richard Middleton

ACKNOWLEDGMENTS

In previous books, I listed each person by name followed by a blurb of thanks. Here I will just list names. Here's what I want to say to you. I love you. I Thank you. I appreciate you. I need you. I'm so blessed to share this journey of life together with you.

I will, however, still give a blurb of thanks to my wife because, compared to anyone else, she stands above and apart in my life. Thank you, my love for standing in my corner through life, through the good, the bad, and the ugly. Thank you for believing in me more than any other human. You've seen me at my best *and* at my worst—repeatedly, and you still stand with me, still believe in me, and still love me like crazy. Your love is precious to me.

Okay, in no order of importance (except my mom), here we go. Mom. Bob. Sis. Logan. Kyla. Grammy. Victoria Barberio. Liz Suarez. Josh Ruby. Chris Mora. Elaine Mora. Val Wells. Clark DeNoon. Lisa Guest. Steve Plummer. Ben and Kristin Koppin. Matt Nugent. Ostap Zabolotnyy. Clarke Brogger. Chris Hedrick. James Mulroney. Sandy Fitzpatrick. Ieda Grigg. The Dangerous Stallion Posse. Voyagers Bible Church. The City of Hope Cancer Treatment Center. Dr. James Waisman.

Thank You!

ABOUT *REBEKAH'S HOPE*

Our passion is to equip those fighting cancer, illness, and despair find hope and healing through our books, videos, e-courses, and apparel.

For more hope-filled resources, visit https://www.rebekahshope.org/

To learn how to write and publish your first book, visit https://www.newbiebookwriter.com/

SPEAKING INQUIRES: Joel is a speaker and teacher, and would love to speak at your church, school, or organization! Rebekah is also excited to share her story and testimony in the same venues. And, of course, they love speaking together.

AUTHOR CONTACT: contact@rebekahshope.org

Made in the USA
Middletown, DE
23 December 2020

28103037R00150